Historical Scripts

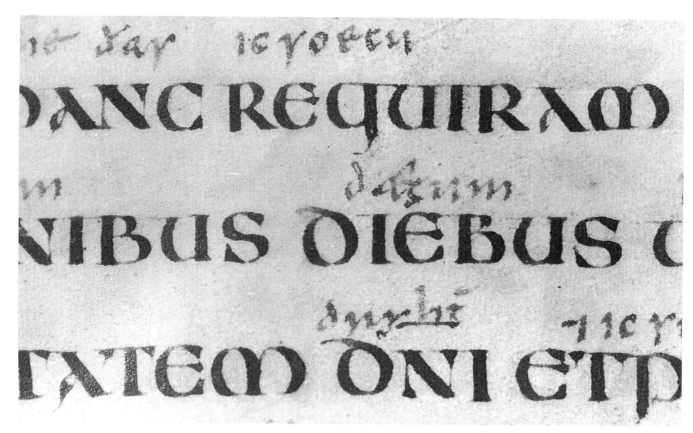

Frontispiece British Library, Cotton Ms. Vespasian A. i. This detail from folio 31R is reproduced at four times actual size. The superb photograph was taken by Nicholas Biddulph. It vividly shows the quality of the ink, the scraped surface of the vellum, and even the granular nature of the gilding. An enlargement of this quality is certainly as good as, if not better than, studying the original manuscript. Astonishingly, this photograph was taken through the glass of a display case in the British Library. Museum photographers, please take note!

To Barbara

Historical Scripts

FROM CLASSICAL TIMES TO THE RENAISSANCE

very best wishes

Stan Knight

Stan Knight

Oak Knoll Press
John Neal, Bookseller
2003

Historical Scripts
was published in 2003 by
Oak Knoll Press
310 Delaware Street
New Castle, Delaware 19720 USA
and:
John Neal, Bookseller
1833 Spring Garden Street
Greensboro, North Carolina 27403 USA

Second, corrected edition, 2003

ISBN: 1-884718-56-6

Book design: Stan Knight & Marcia Friedman
Publication Director: John von Hoelle

Library of Congress Cataloging-in-Publication Data

Knight, Stan.
  Historical Scripts: From Classical Times to the Renaissance
  Stan Knight – 2nd corrected edition
        p. cm.
  Includes bibliographical references (p.108) and index (p.110).
  ISBN 1-884718-56-6 (Hardcover)
  1. Calligraphy – Handbooks, manuals, etc.
  2. Palaeography – Europe – Handbooks, manuals, etc.   I. Title.
  Z43.K65 1998   98-13531
  745.6'1 – DC21   CIP

Printed in the United States of America

Contents

Acknowledgements

In preparing the original edition of *Historical Scripts,* I acknowledged my indebtedness to Julian Brown, then Professor of Palaeography at King's College, London. I was grateful, not only for his lecture series, 'Papyrus, Parchment, Paper' which was hugely informative, but also for his personal generosity in commenting on my raw text in minute detail. His untimely death has been a great loss to the academic world, and I have sorely missed his wise counsel and gentle spirit while preparing this new, enlarged, edition.

So I have been especially thankful to have had the enthusiastic support of Ewan Clayton. Our transatlantic internet discussions have always been both stimulating and entertaining. His opinions and scholarly advice I hold in the highest regard. I am honoured that he consented to contribute a Foreword to my book.

Michelle Brown of the British Library, Christopher de Hamel and his colleagues at Sotheby's, and Alison Sproston of Trinity College, Cambridge have all been extravagantly helpful, attending to the hailstorm of my irritating and persistent requests with utter graciousness.

I received much valuable information for the first edition of *Historical Scripts* from Professor Bernhard Bischoff and Vera Law (who, sadly, have both since died); and from Nicholas Biddulph, Ann Camp, Ewan Clayton and Alison Urwick. Since that time, many others have kindly given encouragement and offered their advice. In particular, Rutherford Aris of the University of Minnesota, David Ganz (who has now succeeded Julian Brown at King's College), and James Mosley of the St Bride Printing Library in London have been most unselfish in sharing their knowledge with me.

My appreciation is due to helpful and patient staff in libraries and museums around the world, especially to Michael Boggan of the British Library Photographic Services, Dr Paul Roberts and his colleague, Andy Meadows, of the British Museum, Dr Cornel Dora of the Stiftsbibliothek at St Gallen, Dr Frauke Steenbock, Curator Emeritus of the Staatliche Museen zu Berlin, Julie Mellby of the Houghton Library at Harvard, and Eric Kindel of the Central Lettering Record in London. In addition, I reiterate my thanks to those who gave of their time and efforts aiding the preparation of the first edition – Janet Backhouse and J P Hudson of the British Library, Bruce Barker-Benfield of the Bodleian Library, Rowan Watson and Vera Kaden of the Victoria & Albert Museum, John Simmons of the Codrington Library, All Souls College, Oxford, and François Avril of the Bibliothèque Nationale, Paris.

Nicholas Biddulph, although now retired from the Central Lettering Record, has kindly provided many of his outstanding photographs of manuscripts and inscriptions for this book. These greatly enhance the quality of illustrations shown here, and set standards for others to reach.

My debt to numerous scholarly authors is acknowledged in the Select Bibliography. Without the magnificent work of scholars such as E A Lowe, a project such as this would be impossible. This bibliography has been much expanded for the second edition. Dozens of new books on calligraphy, typography and palaeography have appeared since 1984.

I am most grateful to Marcia Friedman, whose exacting standards and meticulous attention to detail produced a typographic design worthy of the superb historical manuscripts which are celebrated in these pages. My thanks also to Linnea Lundquist for her phenomenally microscopic scrutiny of the typesetting.

Finally, my loving appreciation to Denys, my wife, for her long-suffering and patience, during the seemingly endless months of deep (and isolating) concentration which was needed to bring this work to a successful conclusion.

Stan Knight

Foreword

From its first appearance *Historical Scripts* has appealed to a number of different communities. It is a book for the historian, the palaeographer, the calligrapher, the typographer and anyone with a interest in western lettering and documents. The first edition proved to be popular and accessible; now revised and expanded (32 more pages) with many new photographs of exceptional quality, this volume supersedes the earlier edition.

Originally this book was one of the fruits of a partnership formed with the calligraphic community by the late Julian Brown, Professor of Palaeography at King's College, London. Generously, he opened his tutorials and lectures to a number of interested scribes. He encouraged us to learn and venture opinions. He believed that the greatest privilege given to the teacher of a subject such as his was the chance to enlarge the lives of his pupils by enriching one of their faculties, 'the sparkling faculty of sight'. He valued his association with calligraphers because we gave him another way of seeing things. It is this way of looking, the maker's way, which Stan Knight's book presents.

The presentation

By illustrating a selection of manuscripts in full page view, with enlargements, and a fragment at actual size, Stan Knight enables us not only to survey the history of bookhands but to see details of letter construction, to make judgements about the technical conditions of writing, its qualities of rhythm and movement, that are usually only possible when consulting an original manuscript. From such observations we can build a subtle and rounded picture of an individual scribe's writing, whilst also creating the potential for our own understanding to become an active and embodied one. The author has gone to considerable lengths to obtain photographs that are appropriately focused and lit so that the tactile qualities of surfaces, ink tone, and flow, are revealed. Some libraries have understood his requests others have not. Many institutions appear unused to photographing manuscripts as artefacts that record the dynamics of a human performance; they expect only to supply a readable copy of the text.

Another unique aspect of this book is its choice of sources. No selection is neutral and Stan has chosen with the eye of a craftsperson and teacher. He has been concerned to find examples of formal writing that show a coherent and reasonably consistent relationship between methods of tool use and letter formation; this makes the construction of a script much easier to grasp in practice. He has also tried to select writing without pronounced idiosyncrasies of style.

So what is it that a calligrapher looks for in a good piece of work? We admire the scribe who embraces writing with an integrated vision, one that extends from the initial contact between pen and page through to the spatial architecture and textural rhythms that find their completion in the finished object. A calligrapher's skill can never be judged on the basis of individual letters, just as musicianship cannot be heard in single notes. A full sense of an individual's vision and mastery of the medium comes from the relationships brought into being between many elements. This is true of calligraphy, as it is true of life.

Occasionally today's artists feel history weighing heavily on their shoulders. Some wish to shake it off and start afresh. But what is the past? It is simply the accumulated experience of generations of people, much like ourselves, who, as James Wardrop expressed it, 'pursued this or that ideal or illusion or appetite and made or unmade themselves in the process'. These largely anonymous men and women offer us models against which we can test our own experience and vision. The thread of connection between us is closer still because written artefacts depend upon shared understandings for their intelligibility. Many of the conventions we use today in letter design and typography were established during the manuscript age. To know the classic work of this period is to know more about the ground we stand upon. If we grasp the context within which this earlier work was conceived, we gain freedom in relation to it; freedom to consciously develop it or to frame an informed reaction to it. In both cases we engage with the layered experience which tradition represents. So we join a great adventure, building a culture, one which makes sense of the human condition and finds shared forms for otherwise raw, chaotic and potentially isolating experiences. This is one justification for working with written artefacts.

Now is an important moment in the history of lettering and documents, perhaps as important as any moment we can identify in the story this book traces. Our technology for producing written artefacts is changing. As it changes many of the structures we have built to bring order to the world of the written word (libraries, publishing houses, the form of the book itself) are being questioned. This brings its own anxiety and disorientation.

The historical continuum

At moments such as these it is helpful to see ourselves as part of a continuum, one that stretches back beyond the age of Gutenberg and the introduction of printing. For historical tradition is never a fixed and immovable force but always a living resource capable of development in new ways. Early printers selected aspects of the manuscript world to build upon, whilst other features, such as complex glossed pages and the many alternative letterforms that solved subtle spacing and textural problems, were neglected. Today we are free to choose from this tradition afresh, selecting for the kinds of artefacts that the new electronic media can fashion. For this reason we need, yet again, the entire history of writing and documents held up before us as we work. *Historical Scripts*, with its survey of the development of bookhands, its excellent illustrations and soundly researched sources, makes an important contribution to this effort, one which is absolutely central to the culture (that enlargement of human experience) which we continue to create.

Ewan Clayton
Sussex, England
on the feast of St Wulstan, 1998

Introduction

CALLIGRAPHY IN HISTORY

A vital rôle

The craft of calligraphy has a two thousand-year history in the Western world. Up to the time of the Renaissance, calligraphy was the only means of preserving literature, and so it played a vital rôle in the spread of learning, culture and religion. The modern calligrapher would be very foolish to ignore the methods, skills and attitudes of generations of historical scribes who produced outstandingly accomplished work for so many centuries.

Since that time, we have hardly improved on the basic, simple tools used almost from the outset: vellum, quills and carbon-based ink.

The basic tools

Early in the Christian era, the preparation and use of membrane (calf or sheep skin) had become common practice in manuscript work. Small parchment fragments found at Dura, however, are thought to date from as early as *c.*100 BC. Papyrus, a writing material made from the sedge plant which grew abundantly in ancient Egypt, had already been in use in the Eastern Mediterranean from the 4th or 3rd millenium BC. The famous Qumrân Scrolls (some as early as the 3rd century BC) were, like many Hebrew rolls, actually written on membrane prepared in the same manner as leather.

The Arabs learned of paper from the Chinese, as early as the 8th century AD, but it was not manufactured in Italy before *c.*1230. Paper was not used extensively for making books until the 15th century. Significantly, only one manuscript in this present collection is written on paper *(F10)*. The development of printing in the mid 15th century stimulated the greater use of paper. Vellum was too expensive for all but the most luxurious printed books.

In general use, the quill probably replaced the rather stiffer reed pen as early as the 6th century AD and, when properly prepared and cut, has proved to be the ideal writing instrument. In medieval times the quill would have been made from the outer wing feathers of a large bird such as a goose or swan. Turkey quills, popular with scribes today, were not used by medieval scribes. Turkeys were native to North America and therefore unknown in Europe before the 16th century.

The use of carbon-based ink stretches from ancient Egyptian times to the 12th century AD. Finely ground charcoal or lamp-black, when mixed with gum water, produced a dense, black pigment. Ink made from iron gall was used as early as the 3rd century AD. This is a more translucent, brown-black ink and can be made by combining oak galls (which contain tannic acid) with copperas (ferrous sulphate). While carbon inks predominated in early medieval times, almost all manuscripts made in the 13th to the 15th centuries were written with iron-gall ink.

The earliest known use of the codex (a manuscript in book form) was in the late 1st or early 2nd century AD. Later, in the 4th and early 5th centuries, much literature previously written on papyrus rolls was transferred to the new codex form, and written on vellum. Since that time, the basic construction of the book has altered very little.

Demise and reinstatement

Calligraphy, as a means of making books, was superseded late in the 15th century by the printing press. In 1480, Sinibaldi, a professional scribe, complained that the invention of printing had so reduced his work, that he hardly earned enough to pay for his clothing! One positive feature of this upheaval, however, was that the early printers made a great deal of use of the skills of the calligrapher. Some of the typefaces were designed by scribes, the layout of the manuscript book was retained, identical parchment or paper was used and printed books were often illuminated or rubricated by hand.

Sadly, calligraphy thereafter degenerated into novelty and ornamentation. Most of the old manuscript skills were lost, virtually for four hundred years. At the beginning of the 20th century, Edward Johnston was the scribe who retraced the medieval approach to the craft, 'rediscovered' the edged pen and provided a foundation on which modern calligraphy could be built.

THE DEVELOPMENT OF SCRIPTS

Continuous change

It is important to understand that historical scripts were not rigidly-fixed 'styles' (as are the majority of modern typefaces). Those illustrated in this book represent the high peaks in an endlessly shifting landscape.

Throughout the centuries, styles of writing were continually being modified and developed. A multitude of influences – political, religious, aesthetic, intellectual, sociological, or pragmatic – wrought changes in the way that books were made and scripts were written. Usually, these changes took place gradually and imperceptibly. Only rarely were

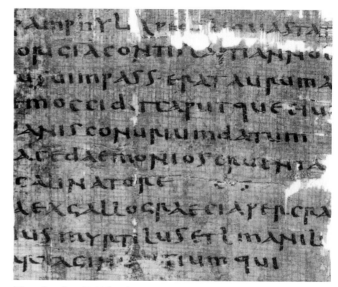

Fig. 1 London, British Library, Papyrus 1532, part of column 1 (actual size). One of 8 fragments of Livy's *Epitome* found at Oxyrhynchus. Mixed script, early 3rd century AD, probably written in Egypt.

writing styles *deliberately* re-formed. The 3rd century papyrus *(Fig. 1)* shows a hand in the very process of development. It is an early appearance of forms characteristic of later Half-uncial scripts (eg. **d, m, p, q** and **r**) and, at the same time, forms similar to the later Uncial letters (**A, E, G, N, S** and **U**) – some of them revealing Greek influence (eg. **A** and **E**).

Fig. 2 London, British Library, Papyrus 745, a fragment of *De Bellis Macedonicis* (actual size). The recto of the parchment *(not* papyrus) found at Oxyrhynchus. This very early script is a formal, literary version of Old Roman Cursive. Transliteration: TUM IMPERI / UE PRAEFECTI / SATIS POLLERENT / US ATQUE ANTIOC / NERIS DESPECTI / ESQUE ALIENAS / CTARENT / PHILIPPU / ONE ANT / VALIDI

Even where vigorous and sustained manuscript production in one centre resulted in a discernable 'house style' (like that at St Martin's in Tours during the first half of the 9th century, or that at Christ Church, Canterbury during the 12th century) the script still varied a little from scribe to scribe, and over the decades even more distinct changes can be discerned.

Causes of change

What caused an established script to change its character? There are at least four different circumstances which could account for script modification.

1 A cursive hand, used for documents or correspondence, might be elaborated or formalized for use as a book script. The fragment of parchment *(Fig. 2)* reveals a very early Latin bookhand which derives a lot of its letterforms from the documentary script called Old Roman cursive *(Fig. 3)*. Compare the two scripts, and note the similarity of the forms of **A, C, D, M, N, P** (which looks like a narrow, rectangular C), **Q** and **U**. Many of the characteristics of Old Roman cursive are also found in early Uncial scripts (see *B6* and *B7*). Note, for example, how in both scripts the upper

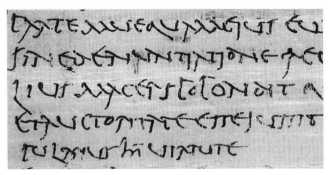

Fig. 3 London, British Library, part of Papyrus 229R, (four-fifths actual size). A deed recording the purchase of a slave boy, dated 24 May AD 166. Written in Old Roman cursive. Transliteration: PARTEMUE QUAM EIUS EV / SINE DENUNTIATIONE REC / LIUS MACER SPOPONDIT Q / ET AUCTORITATE ESSE IUSSIT / PULARIUS iii VIRTUTE

part of the letter E is added to the lower part.

New Roman cursive *(Fig. 4)* was the 'everyday' handwriting of late Antiquity. This was a quickly-written hand incorporating many ligatures and loops, and it formed the basis for many of the Regional hands which emerged in the 5th century AD as the Roman Empire declined. It was also influential in the formation of Roman Half-uncial (see *C1*), especially in its 'lower-case' aspect.

2 A formal script, written very quickly, might eventually break down into a more cursive style, often losing legibility in the process. In such a way, Old Roman cursive *(Fig. 3)* incorporated many ancient Rustic capital forms *(Fig. 7)*.

3 Over the course of time, even a formal script might gradually evolve into a different 'style'. Such a transition can be traced in the development of Uncial scripts. The earlier examples (see *B6–B8*) have simple, lightweight forms, vigorously written with a slanted pen angle. Gradually, later Uncial forms (see *B9–B10*), written with a flattened pen angle, become more ponderous and more complicated.

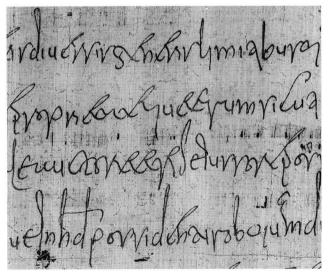

Fig. 4 London, British Library, part of Papyrus 138R, (three-fifths actual size). Fragment of a deed recording a purchase of land, *c.* AD 166. Written in New Roman cursive. Transliteration: s diversis generis limitibusq / proprietateque earum sicuti / le auctore et fideiussore pos / ue in h d possidentur ob quam d

9

Fig. 5 Paris, Bibliothèque Nationale, Ms. Lat. 11641, part of folio 7v (actual size). One of four papyrus fragments of the works of Augustine in a bi-folium of parchment. First five lines Uncials, the remainder Half-uncials, 7th or 8th century AD, written at Luxeuil.

Fig. 6 London, British Library, Add. Ms. 9350, part of folio 208R (actual size). Psalter, with interlinear commentary, written in northern Italy in the 12th century. A handwritten note on folio 1 says, 'Ex hereditate Nicolia de Nicolis de Florentia'.

The metamorphosis from the round, open Caroline minuscule to the heavy angularity of the Gothic scripts can be readily appreciated by studying the evolution of individual letters, such as **o** and **n**, in *C5–C8* and *D1–D5*.

In these periods of change, many scribes would be familiar with more than one 'style' of writing. The Luxeuil manuscript *(Fig. 5)* demonstrates this familiarity: the scribe moves, with ease, from Uncial to Half-uncial script, without even changing his pen!

4 Occasionally, in the course of history, an earlier form of script might be deliberately revived. When it happened, it was usually for philosophical or aesthetic reasons. The use of Square capitals in 9th-century Carolingian manuscripts, for example, was an overt expression of admiration for the glories of ancient Rome (see *E1, E2*).

Then again, at the beginning of the 15th century, Renaissance scholars like Poggio Bracciolini and Niccolò Niccoli developed what we now call Humanist minuscule (see *F3–F5*). Despising the appearance of the Gothic scripts of northern Europe, they turned for their inspiration to the *litera antiqua,* the earlier Italian Caroline minuscule scripts like that shown in *C9.* Niccoli himself owned at least one such 12th-century example, a manuscript now in the collection of the British Library *(Fig. 6).*

Some misconceptions cleared up

Part of the aim of this book is to provide palaeographical information which is not only of help to the calligrapher, but is also as up-to-date and as accurate as possible. The student is not served well by the nonchalant repetition of unsubstantiated ideas.

The first Roman bookhand. It has long been assumed that Rustic capitals were a degenerate form of written Square capitals, compressed to save space. But the earliest examples of Rustics pre-date known examples of written Square capitals by more than three hundred years. While the Gallus papyrus *(Fig. 7)* may not be as ancient as was once thought, there are a number of other manuscript fragments written in Rustic capitals which can, with certainty, be dated to the 1st century AD. Square capitals may indeed be the most impressive Latin bookhand but, undoubtedly, Rustic capitals came first.

Uncials and Half-uncials. When the term 'Half-uncials' was first coined, it was probably thought that, historically, such scripts were a derivation of Uncials. In fact, despite the similarities apparent in certain later manuscripts (see *Fig. 5*), the two scripts developed independently.

Early forms of Uncials (eg. *B6*) evolved from scripts like that of the *De Bellis* fragment *(Fig. 2)*. This has some discernible Uncial characteristics, although it may well have been written as early as AD 100 (see Jean Mallon, *Paléographie Romaine*). Both the *De Bellis* script and early Uncial hands were written with a 'natural' (slanted) pen angle.

Early Half-uncials (eg. *C1*), however, derive from such scripts as that of the Livy *Epitome (Fig. 1)*. Not only do they have certain letterforms in common (ascending **b** and **d**, 'minuscule' **m**, 'capital' **N**, and descending **p** and **q**), but also both scripts were written with a flattened pen angle.

Fig. 7 (above) Saqqara, Egyptian Exploration Society, a fragment of *Elegiacs* by Gallus (actual size). Part of the papyrus fragments found at Quaṣr Ibrîm. Ancient Rustic script. Thought by P J Parsons *(Journal of Roman Studies,* Volume 69) to have been written *c.* 22 BC.

Fig. 8 (below) Bamberg, Staatsbibliothek, Ms. Patr. 87 (B. iv. 21), part of folio 79v (actual size). Works of Jerome and Augustine. Square capitals, 6th century AD, written in southern Italy. The cursive gloss was added in the 8th century.

Compound-stroke capitals. The use of classical Roman capitals was a distinctive feature of Carolingian manuscripts of the 9th century (see *E1* and *E2*), but this was not the first time that such compound-stroke letters had been used. The 6th-century Codex Bambergensis *(C1)* contains a number of colophons and headings in Square capitals, some directly written, but some 'built up' *(Fig. 8)*. However, the earliest example is probably the Trent manuscript known as the Codex Palatinus, dating from the 5th century AD *(Fig. 9)*. These large initials, with their curious serifs, are similar to the 4th-century inscriptional letters of Pope Damasus (see Stanley Morison, *Politics and Script,* plate 68).

SELECTING SCRIPTS FOR THIS BOOK

The next best thing

Ideally, one should study historical scripts at first hand. The originals have a subtlety, fineness and an 'atmosphere' which cannot be captured in reproduction. But access to such manuscripts is often difficult. The documents are, by nature and age, fragile, and the libraries which house them

(quite sensibly) limit their availability even to those engaged in serious research. This book aims to provide the next best thing to studying original manuscripts.

The reproductions have not been chosen at random. A great deal of care has been exercised in selecting the finest available examples of the major bookhands used from Roman times up to the Renaissance. The manuscripts illustrated in this book have a calligraphic coherence which is certainly not to be found in *all* historical scripts.

In the Irish manuscript of the 8th century, for example, we are confronted with a hand which, by modern calligraphic standards, is extremely unsure of itself *(Fig. 10)*. Uncial-like forms (**D** in line 3; **F** line 8, **N** line 6; **R** line 9; **S** line 3) are mixed with Half-uncial (**a** in line 1; **d** line 9; **e** line 5; **m** line 4; **r** line 1; long **s** line 2; **t** line 1), and the whole is written with an Insular 'accent' (see especially **b** in line 1; **f** line 5; **g** line 6; **l** line 3 and **N** line 10).

The selection concentrates on the calligraphic development of mainstream bookhands. Local 'dialects' (such as the Merovingian, Luxeuil, Visigothic, Beneventan minuscules and other idiosyncratic scripts) have been excluded. (For

11

Fig. 9 London, British Library, Add. Ms. 40107, part of folio IV (actual size). One leaf, a fragment of Matthew's Gospel, from the main manuscript which is in the Museo Nazionale, Trento, Italy. Silver Capitals and Uncials on purple vellum, 5th century AD, written in all probability in Africa.

examples of these see Michelle Brown, *A Guide to Western Historical Scripts).*

Since there are a number of similar manuscripts for each individual 'style', it has often been necessary to choose just one as the clearest example. Inevitably, there is some overlap with other published collections such as *The Book of Scripts* by Alfred Fairbank and the plates in *Writing & Illuminating, & Lettering* (Edward Johnston had a particularly discerning eye). Nevertheless, considerable research – much of it new – has been undertaken for the purpose of this volume. Many of the manuscripts illustrated here are not readily accessible anywhere else, especially in this format.

As far as was practical, each original manuscript was examined in order to identify the strongest and clearest pages for reproduction. Some otherwise excellent pages in certain manuscripts are in a poor state of preservation and so, unfortunately, are not suitable.

Admittedly, some of the final choices had to be made 'realistically'. The majority of the examples are from libraries in Britain, which is by no means as restricting as it may seem: the British Library, for example, has one of the finest collections of Western manuscripts in the world. Some manuscripts have proved extremely elusive: a 15-year search for the Humanist script which Edward Johnston showed as Figs. 175 and 176 in *Writing & and Illuminating, & Lettering* has been in vain.

But others were delightful 'discoveries' – a dozen or more manuscripts of very high quality which were unknown, at least to me! Most, in the course of research, emerged 'by chance', and caught me by surprise; among them the Arundel and Amesbury Psalters, the Trinity Gospels, the Tours Bibles at Munich and Paris, the Bodleian Uncial, and the two Yates Thompson Books of Hours.

The format of this handbook

For ease of study, each manuscript is featured on its own spread, so that illustrative material can be seen adjacent to information relevant to each example.

The notes on each manuscript are by no means exhaus-

tive, but clear identification is given to enable further research. Background information is provided where it seems to me relevant or interesting. The qualities and importance of each example are discussed in relation to other, similar manuscripts; particular difficulties in writing the hand are indicated.

A full page from each manuscript is shown, with complete margins, to put the script in its proper context. It should be noted, however, that most medieval manuscripts have been rebound at least once since they were first written, and their margins may now be somewhat smaller than was originally intended.

A large-scale section of each manuscript is included to facilitate easier analysis and clearer understanding of the movements of the pen. A detail (at actual size) is provided at the end of each set of notes for ready comparison with the other scripts.

STUDYING HISTORICAL SCRIPTS

Some considerations

It must be remembered that none of these scripts – apart from the Cataneo *(F7)* – were ever *intended* as exemplars. Consequently they are not always consistent or 'perfect'. Some measure of understanding is needed if they are to be used as models.

Medieval manuscripts were often written on vellum of varying quality, with a quill pen which was usually more blunt than today's steel pens. Reservoirs were rarely used, the flow of the pen was controlled by adjusting the angle of the writing board and the consistency of the ink. Very *few* historical scripts were written with 'hairline' sharpness. Copying a medieval script with a steel pen on paper can never produce exactly the same 'look'.

Manuscripts were usually ruled with a single line for each line of text (scored with a blunt point, or drawn with plummet or pale ink). This line ruling was not used to control the size of the writing, but as a guide for the number of text lines required on each page. So, naturally, the letter height varied considerably in any given text. Therefore, in order to simulate the actual weight of the original writing, an *average* letter height must be ascertained.

The size and style of a manuscript and its writing were often related to its original purpose. Some manuscripts were intended as prestige documents, made for ceremonial or liturgical use: their pages were large, their decoration elaborate, and their writing big and occasionally heavily serifed. Other, more personal, books used smaller, less formal scripts and were written quickly. Some historical scripts were incredibly small, occasionally even less than 1 mm high (compare *F8*)! This affected the spacing as well as the uniformity and construction of the letters. Size and scale are strong determining factors in the actual design of scripts.

Although the examples in this collection are presented in largely chronological order, it is not the intention that the student should work through in sequence from the first to the last. In fact, some of the earliest scripts are the most difficult to write.

Analysing pen-made letters

There is no point whatever in attempting merely to imitate medieval writing (or any other). Analysis should lead to a clear understanding of how the hand was constructed and written, and to discover the 'spirit' as well as – indeed, rather than – the 'letter' of the original. In this way, historical scripts can be used in contemporary manuscripts in an appropriate manner. It is also possible to 'breed varieties' (as Edward Johnston suggested) from such developed forms; adapting and modifying them according to the demands of the new situation in which they are to be used.

Fig. 10 St Gallen, Stiftsbibliothek, Ms. S.B. 1395, part of folio 446R (actual size). Insular script, 8th century AD, presumably written in Ireland.

The scripts in the reproductions should not be copied by tracing the outlines and 'filling in'. It may, however, be found helpful to follow the enlarged letters with a clean, broad-edged pen of an appropriate size in order to get the feel of the writing and to observe the movements of the pen.

There is no better advice than Edward Johnston's for the analysis of historical scripts (see *Formal Penmanship,* pages 119–121). His seven pen-stroke constants (features normally constant in any manuscript) provide a sure guide to the essential character of any formal script.

There are three features which determine the character of the script: 1 The *Angle* of the edge of the pen to the writing line (which may vary in certain scripts from letter to letter, or even within a single letter). This angle is seen most readily at the beginning and ending of pen strokes or at the thickest parts of curved letters. 2 The *Weight* of the letters, which is conveniently expressed in the relationship of the width of the pen stroke to the height of the letters. The width of the pen being used can usually be seen in heavy diagonal strokes or at the thickest parts of curved letters. 3 The *Shape* or structural form of the letters, commonly determined in minuscule scripts by the shape of the **o** and the **n**. For example, narrow versions of these two letters should result in an alphabet which is compressed throughout.

Three features concern the construction of the letters: 4 The *Number,* 5 the *Order,* and 6 the *Direction* of the pen strokes which are needed for the formation of individual letters. Broad-edged pens work best when pulled, downwards or sideways, or when they are slid along their edge, producing 'hairlines'. This means that most written letters (especially larger, more formal ones) should be made with more than one stroke of the pen.

The final feature affects the 'spirit' of the writing: it is, 7 the *Speed* at which the original manuscript was written. Many medieval scribes worked quickly, without hesitation. This speed affected the shapes which could be made by the pen. Really fast scripts would be made less precisely, and they would often incorporate many joins, ligatures and flourishes. Such scripts are commonly described as cursive, literally, 'running'! To capture the true spirit of a script, one should attempt to write at the same speed as the original scribe.

To gain maximum benefit from each of the reproductions of historical manuscripts in this book, the student is advised to study Chapter 6 in Part 1 of *Formal Penmanship* and Chapter 4 in *Writing & Illuminating, & Lettering.*

Stan Knight
Mount Vernon, Washington
on the Eve of St Stephen, 1997

13

Classical Letters

The earliest surviving Greek inscriptions indicate that the Greeks first learnt to write shortly before 750 BC. The tradition that they were taught by the Phoenicians is supported by the similarities between the two scripts. The beginnings of the modern, Western alphabet are clearly discernible in these Greek inscriptions. Indeed, some of the letterforms have not changed at all.

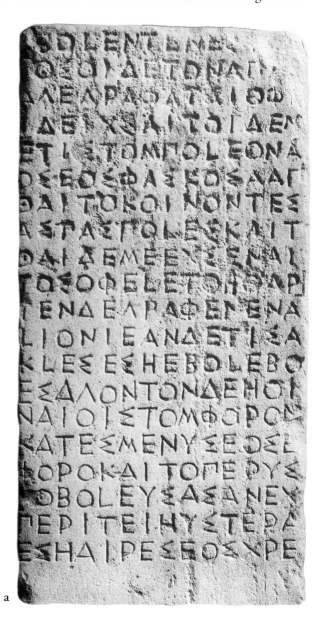

a London, British Museum, BMI 6. Probably, 426–425 BC. Athens, marble stele. Overall size: 20" x 8¼" (51 x 21 cm).

Transliteration of lines 14–18: ESAGONTON DE HOI / NAIOIS TOM PhORON / KA TES MENUSEOS E / PhORO KAI TO PERUS / ROBOLEUSASAN ECh

One of four fragments of a large Decree, the rest of which is in Athens. The Decree concerns the payment of tribute (PhOROS) to the city of Athens. This fragment from the British Museum outlines formal procedures to be followed in cases of dispute over the tribute.

Most Greek inscriptional letters, particularly early ones, are of monoline construction. Following the Phoenician pattern, the Greeks first wrote from right to left. In some later inscriptions, alternate lines ran in opposite directions, like ploughing, an arrangement called *boustrophedon* ('ox turning'). The inscription illustrated here reads from left to right, but has both vertical and horizontal alignment, called *stoichedon* ('in files', like soldiers on parade). This arrangement is made easier because most letters are of the same width. No word spaces are used, and many words are arbitrarily split at the ends of lines. Note the archaic forms of gamma (Λ), lambda (L), and pi (Γ), and that no distinction is made between eta (long E) and epsilon (short E).

b London, British Museum, BMI 399. 334 BC. Inscription from the temple of Athena, Priene. Overall size: 19¼" x 48" (50 cm x 122 cm).

Transliteration: BASILEUS ALEXANDROS / ANEThĒKE TON NAON / AThĒNAIĒI POLIADI. The inscription reads 'King Alexander dedicated the temple to Athena Polias'.

These majestic letters are of monoline construction and 'square' proportion. They exhibit what is perhaps the earliest attempt at serifing; this is particularly noticeable at the end of line 1, in the word 'ALEXANDROS'. Note the continued use of the archaic form of pi (Γ), but the distinction made between epsilon (E) and eta (H).

a

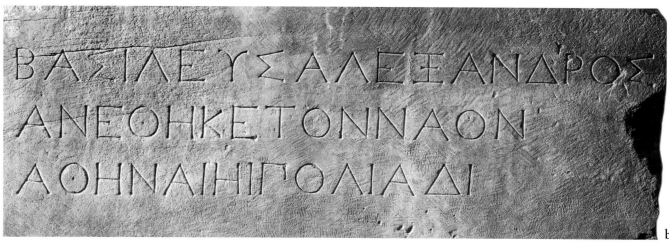

b

c

c London, British Museum, BMI 171. AD 143. From a Roman
gateway at Thessalonica in northern Greece. Overall size:
32¾" x 70¾" (83 x 180 cm).

Transliteration of lines 1 and 2: POLEITARChOUNTŌN
SŌSIPATROU TOU KL(EO) / PATRAS KAI LOUKIOU
PONTIOU SEKOUNDO(U)

The inscription lists names of those who held public
office in Thessalonica at that time. 'Politarchs' (line 1, literally 'rulers of the citizens') was a peculiar title, used in only
a few Greek cities. Its use in Thessalonica is confirmed in
the New Testament (Acts of the Apostles 17: 6).

The letterforms are influenced by Roman inscriptions of
the time. The serifs are fully developed, and there is evidence
of a distinction between thick and thin strokes in certain
places. Some triangular word dividers are used here. Note
the decorative crossbar on **A**, and that the central crossbars
on **E** and **H** do not always connect. The letter height changes
after line 4 and occasionally, to achieve a letter fit, the letters
are compressed. Originally, several lines of text had letters
which ran onto an adjacent stone. **EO** is missing from the
end of line 1 and **Y** from the end of line 2.

d London, British Museum, BMI 928. 2nd century AD.
From the base of a statue in the city of Miletus. Overall
size: 32½" x 14½" (82.5 x 37 cm).

Transliteration of lines 1–5: AGATHĒ TUChĒ / LEUKION
LEUKI / OU NIKĒSANTA / TA MEGALA DIDU / MEIA
AGŌNISA

The Council and People of Miletus honour an athlete,
Lucius, son of Lucius, for his victory in the Great Didymaean
Games and for competing in the Olympic Games at Pisa.

The letterforms on this inscription are rather decorative
in character. They incorporate heavy, triangular serifs and
distinctive forms of rho (**P** line 8, letter 4), phi (**Φ** line 8,
letter 12), and omega (**Ω** line 5, letter 7). Note the **ME**
ligature and tiny **O** (line 9) used to save space, and the **NE**
ligature (line 12). No consistent word spaces are used, and
many words are arbitrarily split at the ends of lines.

d

SENATVS·POPVL
IMP·P·CAESARI·DIV
TRAIANO·AVG·GE
MAXIMO·TRIB·POT
ADDECLARANDVM·Q
MONS·ET·LOCVS·TANT

A B D E
M O R S

SQVE·ROMANVS

NERVAE·F·NERVAE

M·DACICO·PONTIF

VII·IMP·VI·COS·VI·P·P

VANTAE·ALTITVDINIS

IBVS·SIT·EGESTVS

Rome, Trajan's Forum. AD 113. Marble panel on the pedestal of Trajan's Column. Overall size (excluding the moulding): 3'9" x 9' (114 x 274 cm).

The inscription and the 100-foot (30 m) carved column commemorate the military victories of the Emperor Trajan. The inscription, set at the top of the column's 15-foot (4.5 m) pedestal, was defaced in the 9th or 10th century to accommodate a V-shaped gable placed over a door.

The reproduction of the whole inscription is from the polyester cast made by E M Catich from the original panel in Rome. The cast is now on display in the offices of the Mobium Corporation in Chicago, Illinois. The individual letters are from photographs of the original inscription taken by E M Catich, included as separate plates in his book *The Trajan Inscription in Rome.*

The magnificent letters of this inscription demonstrate that, despite borrowing letterform ideas from the Greeks, it was the Romans who, between the late 1st century BC and the early 2nd century AD, perfected formal monumental lettering. Two thousand years later, the classical Roman alphabet

still remains the criterion for evaluating lettering quality.

Note the subtle use of shading and entasis on the stems of the letters; their elegant weight and graceful serifs; their carefully balanced proportions; and the generous, even spacing. All these qualities combine to form a beautiful, harmonious and supremely legible inscription.

Note also the changes of letter size. Lines 1 and 2 are 4½" (115 mm) high; lines 3 and 4, 4⅜" (111 mm); line 5, 4⅛" (105 mm); and line 6, 3⅞" (98 mm). When viewed from ground level, all the lines appear to be of the same height. The backward tilt given to curves and the disposition of thick and thin strokes betray the probable use of a square-ended brush in (quite rapidly) planning out the inscription before it was incised into the marble, 'the cutting being merely a fixing, as it were, of the writing', (W R Lethaby's Preface to *Writing & Illuminating, & Lettering).* Recent research by Tom Perkins *(The Trajan Secrets),* suggests the possible use of a refined, geometric framework for the letter proportions. Roman inscriptions were usually completed with a layer of minium, a colour similar to burnt sienna, painted in the incised letters.

b

The Trajan inscription is justly famous, but it is not the only example of the excellence of Roman monumental lettering. Each of the individually distinctive inscriptions shown in both *A3* and *A4* demonstrates Roman pre-eminence. They illustrate the power and influence of Roman culture, even to the extremes of the Empire.

a Rome, by the Via Appia (still in situ). 1st or 2nd century AD. Overall size (excluding the moulding): probably about 6' x 9' (*c.*183 x 274 cm).

Despite the ravages of time, this inscription retains something of its original grandeur. It was an enormous undertaking (a rough estimate suggests that it had all of 500 letters), yet it is superbly consistent, and must have required much pre-planning with a broad, flat brush. Without abbreviations or word-splitting at the end of lines (compare *A4)*, each of the 16 long lines has been accurately centered, necessitating the use of something like typographic 'justification'. See the very close spacing and narrower letters of line 11, and the openness of line 12. However, the enlargement shows that the precision and regularity have not 'killed' the letterform; on the contrary, it is full of energy and character (see the powerful **Q**).

  Note that the inscription is more deeply cut and of heavier weight than the Trajan, and that **A**, **M** and **N** have flattened, serifed tops.

b London, British Museum, CIL III 6580. AD 194. From Alexandria in northern Egypt. Overall size: 26" x 29" (66 x 74 cm).

This is a military inscription dedicated to the Emperor Septimius Severus. While lacking the outstanding quality of the other, more formal, inscriptions shown here, this example reveals a well-judged relationship between the two styles of letters used. Square capitals are reserved for the important opening words and Rustic capitals used for the remainder (compare the written form of Rustic capitals in *B2)*. The size/weight ratio between them is finely resolved.

  The incised Rustic capitals clearly betray their pen-made character; undoubtedly, the words were first drafted onto the stone with a broad, flat brush. The letter cutter, perhaps inexperienced, has copied the marks without attempting to improve them. This has resulted in vigorous, but rather casual letters, especially the somewhat 'loose' forms of **F** and **S**.

  Note the imperfections in the Square capitals: the strangely weighted **M**, the top-heavy **E**, the backward sloping **S** and the uneven spacing of the first seven letters – the last three seem to be almost an afterthought. Maybe the original intention was to centre the words, 'IMP CAES' (which was a usual abbreviation, see *A4)*. When this did not work out, perhaps the other letters were added in an attempt to remedy the situation.

Shrewsbury, Rowley's House Museum. AD 130. From the Forum Viroconium, Wroxeter. Overall size (excluding the moulding): 3'6" x 11'4" (107 x 345 cm).

These fragments of a sandstone inscription from the entrance to the Forum at Wroxeter, a Roman settlement near to present-day Shrewsbury, were not found until 1924. The inscription records that the Forum was erected by the Cornovii community during the fourteenth year of the reign of the Emperor Hadrian. Although damaged, it is the largest, and undoubtedly the finest surviving example of Roman monumental lettering in Britain.

It is a majestic inscription. The large capitals measure: line 1, 9¼" (235 mm) high; line 2, 8⅜" (212 mm); line 3, 7½" (191 mm); line 4, 6¾" (172 mm); and line 5, 6" (153 mm). The letters are light in weight, perhaps because they are so tall. The ratio of the main letter strokes to the letter height is approximately 1:11. Smaller classical Roman capitals are somewhat heavier. The Appian Way letters *(A3a)*, which are almost 3" (76 mm) tall, have a ratio of approximately 1:7. The capitals from the Trajan Column *(A2)*, the largest of which are just 4½" (115 mm) high, have a ratio of approximately 1:10.

The individual proportions of the Wroxeter capitals also differ a little from those of the Trajan inscription. Note the small upper bowl of **B**, **P**, and **R**; the long, low central bar of **E**; the narrow **N**, the top-heavy **S**; and the wide **X**.

Overall, these letters appear rather stiff and rigid. Unlike the Trajan capitals, the straight strokes have little or no entasis, their sides are quite parallel. Many of their curved letters seem to be constructed geometrically. Their serifs are very flat. Richard Grasby *(The Making of Two Roman Inscriptions)* sees evidence of incised outlines, both straight and curved. These suggest that these capitals were planned out with a stylus and ruler, and some form of compass, rather than with a flat brush. In his article Grasby also considers the use of geometric guidelines for the layout of this inscription, and for that at Caerleon.

Note the pointed tops of **A**, **M**, and **N**, the ligatured **TH** (at the end of line 1) and **NT** (line 3); the 'ivy leaf' and 'clover leaf' (line 1) word dividers; and the random splitting of words at the end of lines.

PROXIMA CIRCAEAE RADUNTUR LITORA TERRAE
DIUES INACCESSOS UBI SOLIS FILIA LUCOS
ADSIDUO RESONAT CANTU TECTISQ SUPERBIS
URIT ODORATAM NOCTURNA IN LUMINA CEDRUM
ARCUTO TENUIS PERCURRENS PECTINE TELAS
HINC EXAUDIRI GEMITUS IRAEQUE LEONUM
UINCLA RECUSANTUM ET SERA SUB NOCTE RUDENTUM
SAETIGERIQUE SUES ATQUE IN PRAESEPIBUS URSI
SAEUIRE AC FORMAE MAGNORUM ULULARE LUPORUM
QUOS HOMINUM EX FACIE DIA SAEUA POTENTIB HERBIS
INDUERAT CIRCE IN UULTUS AC TERGA FERARUM
QUAE NE MONSTRA PII PATERENTUR TALIA TROES
DELATI IN PORTUS NEU LITORA DIRA SUBIRENT
NEPTUNUS UENTIS IMPLEUIT UELA SECUNDIS
ATQ FUGAM DEDIT ET PRAETER UADA FERUIDA UEXIT
IAM RUBESCEBAT RADIIS MARE ET AETHERIA BALTO
AURORA IN ROSEIS FULGEBAT LUTEA BIGIS
CUM UENTI POSUERE OMNISQUE REPENTE RESIDIT
FLATUS ET IN LENTO LUCTANTUR MARMORE TONSAE
ATQUE HIC AENEAS INGENTEM EX AEQUORE LUCUM
PROSPICIT HUNC INTER FLUUIO TIBERINUS AMOENO

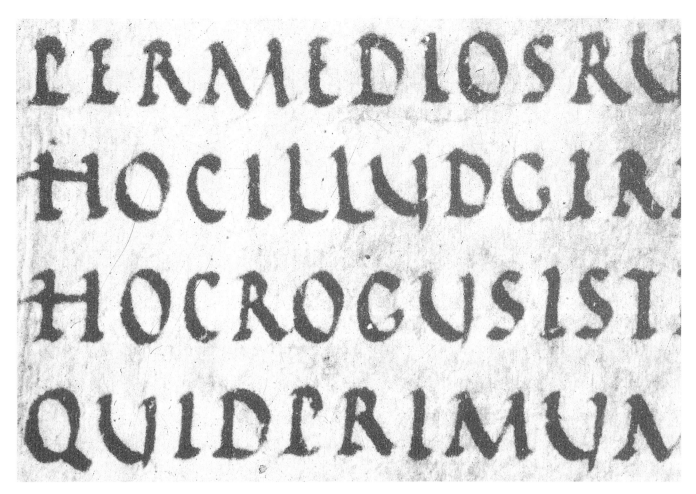

Codex Vaticanus. Rome, Biblioteca Apostolica Vaticana (Vatican Library), Ms. Lat. 3225 (Works of the Latin author, Virgil). Written in Rome, *c.* AD 400.

The page size is now 8⅝" x 7¾" (218 x 197 mm), trimmed from the original size by subsequent re-bindings. The 21 lines of text form a square approximately 6¼" x 6¼" (160 x 160 mm). Originally there were probably some 440 folios, of which only 75 folios remain. The whole-page reproduction (actual size) is taken from folio 58v, and the enlargement (four times actual size) is from folio 41v, lines 6–9.

The first Roman bookhand was Rustic capitals. There are a number of other manuscripts written in Rustics, which can, with certainty, be assigned to the 1st century AD. Rustic capitals, therefore, pre-date known examples of written Square capitals by more than 300 years.

Rustic capitals were used in the 1st century AD throughout the Roman empire for books and formal documents. They continued to be used for literary manuscripts, especially for the works of Virgil, until the 6th century AD. Later, Rustics were used by scribes (up to the onset of the Gothic period) for 'display' purposes: headings, introductions, prefaces, etc. (see *B10, C6* and *C8).* Painted Rustics, such as those at Pompeii, first appeared in the 1st century AD, carved Rustic capitals (see *A3b)* perhaps not until the 2nd century.

Codex Vaticanus is just one of a number of impressive Rustic manuscripts which have survived from the Late

Antique period. Its 'square' text layout, generous margins, precisely-formed and openly-spaced script written on thin, high-quality sheepskin, together with the 50 surviving miniature paintings, distinguishes it as a luxury edition of the Virgil text. However, overall, the format is of modest size and scale. Just one scribe wrote the whole of the text in oak gall ink, with the occasional use of vermilion.

This 'style' of Rustic capitals, which is distinctly different from that of the Palatinus *(B2),* was copied by Anglo-Saxon and Carolingian scribes of the 8th and 9th centuries. The Rustics on the preliminary pages of the Vespasian Psalter (fols. 4–11), and especially those of the Utrecht Psalter, closely resemble this Vaticanus script.

This script is less compressed than that of the Palatinus, and its pen angles vary less dramatically. Generally they range from about 70° for some upright strokes to about 50° for diagonals. This results in sturdier, rounder letters.

Note the wideness of **M**, **N** and **U**. The letters **E**, **P**, **R** and **T** are quite narrow. Note the lack of crossbar on **A** (typical of Rustic scripts); the over-long foot serif given to **P**; the alternative tails for **Q**; and the particular form of **U/V** (faithfully followed by the later scribes). The interlinear space is about the same as the letter height, excepting tall **B**, **F** and **L**.

23

v̄

PYRGOTOTPRIAMINATORVMAEGIACONVTRIX·
NONBEROEVOBISNONHAECRHOETEIAMATRES
ESTDORYCLICONIVNXDIVINISIGNADECORIS·
ARDENTISQVENOTATEOCVLOSQVISPIRITVSILLI
QVISVOLTVSVOCISQVESONVSETGRESSVSEVNTI
IPSAEGOMETDVDVMBEROENDIGRAESSARELIQVI
AEGRAAMINDIGNANTEMTALIQVODSOLACARERET
MVNERENECMERITOSANCHISAEINTERREITHONORES·
HAECETTATA·
ADMATRESPRIAMOANCIPITESOCVLISQVEMALIGNIS·
AMBIGVAESPECTARERATESMISERVMINTERAMOREM
PRAESENTISTERRAE·TATISQVEVOCANTIAREGNA·
CVMDEASEPARIBVSPERCAELVMSVSTVLITALIS·
INGENTEMQVEFVGASECVITSVBNVBIBVSARCVM·
TVMVEROATTONITAEMONSTRISACTAEQVEFVRORE
CONCLAMANT·RAPIVNTQVEFOCISPENETRALIBVSIGNEM·
PARSSPOLIANTARASTRONDEMACVIRGVLTATACESQVE
CONICIVNTFVRITINMISSISVOLCANVSHABENIS
TRANSTRAPERETREMOSETPICTASABIETEPVPPES
NVNTIVSANCHISAETTVMVIVMCVNEOSQVETHEATRI·
INCENSASPERTERTNAVISEVMEIVSETIPSI
RESPICIVNTATRAMINNIMBOVOLITARETAVILLAM·
PRIMVSETASCANIVSCVRSVSKILAETVSEQVESTRIS

131

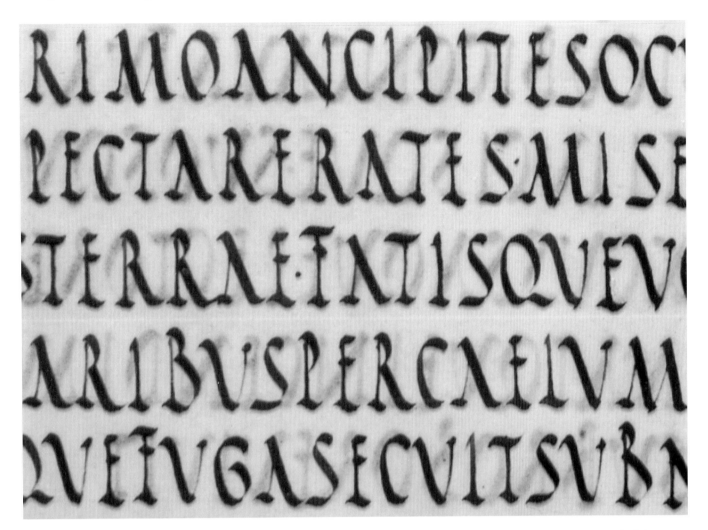

Codex Palatinus. Rome, Biblioteca Apostolica Vaticana (Vatican Library), Ms. Pal. Lat. 1631 (Work of the Latin author, Virgil). Written in Italy. This manuscript is usually assigned to the 4th or 5th century AD, but recent evidence suggests that it is more likely to be a 6th-century copy of an earlier Rustic Virgil.

The page size is 12" x 9¼" (305 x 235 mm); the 23 lines of text take up an area of 8¼" x 7¼" (210 x 185 mm). The manuscript has 256 folios. The whole-page reproduction and the enlargement (three times actual size) are both taken from folio 131R.

Codex Palatinus and Codex Vaticanus *(B1)* are just two of the prestigious manuscripts written in Rustic capitals, surviving from Late Antiquity. Others include Codex Romanus (Vatican, Ms. Lat. 3867), Codex Bembinus (Vatican, Ms. Lat. 3226) and Codex Mediceus (Florence, Biblioteca Medicea-Laurenziana, Ms. Laur. 39. 1 with one leaf in Vatican Ms. Lat. 3225, fol. 76). The Romanus script is closest to the Palatinus 'style'. However, it is less expert than the Palatinus in both letterform and spacing, despite its size. Its capitals are ⅓" (8 mm) high; it is the largest of all the ancient majuscule scripts. The Bembinus and Mediceus scripts are much smaller than the others, and are of the wider, sturdier Vaticanus 'style'.

The Palatinus script is the most sophisticated of the ancient Rustic capitals. Although it has the appearance of an easy, natural and quickly-written hand, this script is extremely difficult to master and should not be attempted by a beginner.

The pen angle varies a great deal – it changes from letter to letter and sometimes even within a single letter. It ranges from approximately 80° for uprights, to 60° for large curved strokes, and to 45° for main diagonals. In addition, there is some use of the corner of the pen in the formation of hairline strokes and serifs.

The narrowness of the letters (especially **E**, **P**, **R** and **T**) is aided by the extremely steep pen angle (possibly helped by a 'left oblique' pen). The impression of compactness is emphasized by close but rhythmical letter spacing and narrow interlinear spaces.

Note the lack of crossbar on **A**; the unusual form of **H**; the parallel strokes of **M** (it appears like two A shapes joined together); and the second, hairline stroke of **V** which consistently is too short at the top.

EFICIVNTAVTVMBRANOCETPATERIPSECOLE(N)DI
HAVDFACILEMESSEVIAMNOLVITPRIMVSQ(VE)PERAR(TE)
MOVITAGROSCVRISACVENSMORTALIACORDA
NECTORPEREGRAVIPASSVSSVAREGNAVETERNO
ANTEIOVEMNVLLISVBIGEBANTARVACOLONI
NESIGNAREQVIDEMAVIPARTIRILIMITECAMPV
EASERATINMEDIVMQVAEREBANTIPSAQ(VE)TELLV(S)
OMNIALIBERIVSNVLLOPOSCENTEFEREBAT
ILLEMALVMVIRVSSERPENTIBADDIDITATRIS
...ENDARIQ(VE)LVPOSIVSSITPONTVMQ(VE)MOVERI
MELLAQ(VE)DECVSSITFOLIISIGNEMQ(VE)REMOVIT
ETPASSIMRIVISCVRRENTIAVINAREPRESSIT
VTVARIASVSVSMEDITANDOEXTVNDERETARTES
PAVLATIMETSVLCISFRVMENTIQVAERERETHERBA
ETSILICISVENISABSTRVSVMEXCVDERETIGNEM
TVNCALNOSPRIMVMFLVVIISENSERECAVATAS
NAVITATVNCSTELLISNVMEROSETNOMINAFECIT
PLEIADASHYADASCLARAMQ(VE)LYCAONISARCTO
TVMLAQVEISCAPTAREFERASETFALLEREVISCO
INVENTVMETMAGNOSCANIB(VS)CIRCVMDARESAL(TVS)

Codex Augusteus. Rome, Biblioteca Apostolica Vaticana (Vatican Library), Ms. Lat. 3256 and Berlin, Deutsche Staatsbibliothek, Cod. Lat. Fol. 416 (Virgil, *Georgics).* Written in Italy, probably in the 4th century AD, though some scholars assign it to the 6th century.

The estimated size of the original page is 16¾" x 12¾" (425 x 325 mm); the 20 lines of text take up an area of 9⅞" x 10½" (250 x 265 mm). Only 7 folios survive of the original manuscript, 4 in the Vatican and 3 in Berlin. The correct order of these remaining fragments would be: Vat. 1, Berl. 1, Vat. 3, Vat. 2, Berl. 2, Vat. 4, Berl. 3. The whole-page reproduction is taken from the Vatican folio 3R, and the enlargement (twice actual size) from the Berlin folio 1R. Both show lines from Virgil's *Georgics.*

Written Square capitals are closely related to inscriptional Roman capitals (see *A2–A4*) in their letterform and spacing, and also in the absence of word separation and punctuation. As the individual letterforms are complicated and time consuming, and as they take up a great deal of space, their use as a bookhand at this time was undoubtedly reserved for prestige manuscripts containing only the most important texts.

This Codex Augusteus and the Codex Sangallensis *(B4)* are the only surviving examples of ancient manuscripts written entirely in Square capitals. Though now in fragments, they show all the characteristics of luxury volumes – a large format with 'square' text block, very generous margins and a meticulously written script. The Vatican leaves, in particular, give a good impression of the original proportions. It is estimated that this copy of the *Georgics* would have taken up as many as 360 folios. Nevertheless, each page is headed

with a large, decorative initial. J J G Alexander *(The Decorated Letter)* suggests that perhaps these are the earliest occurrences of such letters in manuscript use.

The Square capitals of the Codex Augusteus are precisely written and widely spaced, creating a magnificent page. Generally, they follow the character of Roman inscriptional letters, however, **E, F, L,** and **T** are rather narrow for classical proportions. **A** is written without a crossbar, and **R** has an idiosyncratic, thin upright – both features of the earlier *Rustic* capitals.

Many changes of pen angle are required for this script. Overall, the pen angle of the Augusteus is flatter than that of the Sangallensis, but curved strokes and diagonals are written with a slanted pen angle. Upright strokes in **N** and **R** require an almost 90° pen angle. Note the liberal use of pen manipulation and the corner of the pen in the formation of the serifs (see, for example, the 'forked' serifs on **C, G,** and **S).**

The interlinear space is equal to the letter height, excepting the slightly taller **F** and **L.** The smaller letters at the ends of lines perhaps indicate an attempt to follow the exact layout of the manuscript being copied. Characteristics of this script which might be corrected are the over-long foot serifs on **F** and **P,** the slightly top-heavy (almost backward leaning) **S,** and the occasional, over-exuberant extension of the hairline stroke of **V.**

VICIT INTER DURUM PIETAS DATUROR ATUERI

NAT ET UAE T NOTAS AUDIRE ET REDDERE UOCES

SIC EQUIDEM DUCEBAM ANIMO REBARQUE FUTURUM

TEMPORA DINUMERANS NEC ME MEA CURA FEFELLIT

QUAS EGO T ET ERRAS ET QUANTA PER AEQUORA UECTUM

ACCIPIO QUANTIS IACTATUM NATE PERICLIS

QUAM METUI NE QUIT LIBYAE TIBI REGNA NOCERENT

ILLE AUTEM TUA ME GENITOR TUA TRISTIS IMAGO

DESUPER OSTENTAT DE IN SUMMA CACUMINA LINQUNS

SAEPIUS OCCURRENS HAEC LIMINA TENDERE ADEGIT

STANT SALE TYRRHENO CLASSES DA IUNGERE DEXTRAM

DA GENITOR TEQUE AMPLEXU NE SUBTRAHE NOSTRO

SIC MEMORANS LARGO FLETU SIMUL UO RA RIGABAT

TER CONATU SIBI COLLO DARE BRACCHIA CIRCUM

TER FRUSTRA COMPRENSA MANUS EFFUGIT IMAGO

PAR LEVIBUS UENTIS UOLUCRIQUE SIMILLIMA SOMNO

INTEREA UIDET AENEAS IN UALLE REDUCTA

SECLUSUM NEMUS ET UIRGULTA SONANTIA SILUAE

LETHAEUMQUE DOMOS PLACIDAS QUI PRAENATAT AMNEM

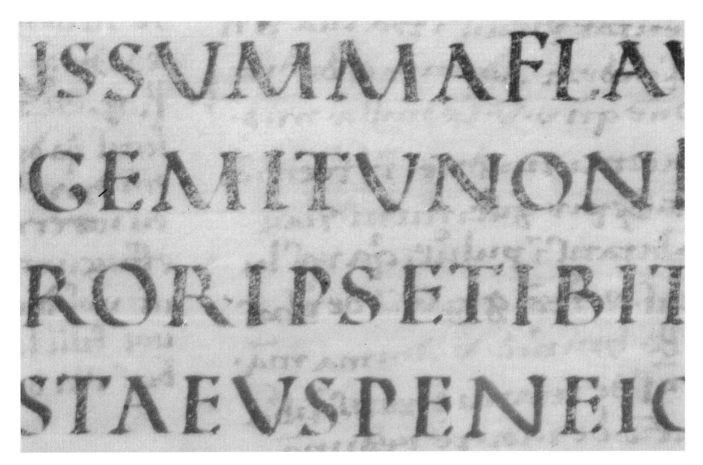

Codex Sangallensis. St Gallen, Stiftsbibliothek, Ms. Cod. 1394, pages 7–48 (Works of Virgil). Written in Italy in the 5th century AD.

The estimated size of the original page is 13½" x 14¾" (340 x 375 mm); the 19 long lines of text take up an area of 8¾" x 10¾" (223 x 275 mm). Only 11 folios remain (most only in part). There are 12 fragments collected, with paper interleaves, between pages 5 and 50 of this codex. (The complete Ms. Cod. 1394 contains fragments of seven other manuscripts.) The whole-page reproduction is taken from page 31 and shows part of the *Aeneid,* and the enlargement (two and a half times actual size) is taken from page 39 showing part of the *Georgics.*

This Codex Sangallensis and the Codex Augusteus *(B3)* are the only surviving examples of ancient manuscripts written entirely in Square capitals. They are extremely complex to write, and thus time consuming and laborious, so it is perhaps not surprising that so few ancient books used Square capitals for the whole of their text. Professor Julian Brown used to joke that 'Square capitals for manuscript use was a late idea and a bad one'! Later scribes avoided them as a bookhand (preferring the more efficient, faster Uncial or Half-uncial scripts), but they did use them occasionally for display headings (see Introduction, *Fig. 8).* The Humanists, however, revived their use (on title pages, for example) and Bartolomeo San Vito made a speciality of them (see *F2).*

The 12 leaves of Codex Sangallensis which survive are badly damaged. Most are severely cropped. Page 31 (oppo-

site) is the only one with the whole of the text area still intact. Many of the seven leaves of the *Aeneid* are indecipherable, and all of the four leaves of the *Georgics* are heavily palimpsest. The original margins were very generous – the largest head margin now (page 7) is 2⅝" (65mm), and the widest foredge margin (page 15) is 3½" (75mm).

Despite the fact that only a handful of pages of this manuscript have survived, slight variations of script style can be detected. Close study reveals at least four different hands at work. (Compare the forms of **M, N, P, R, S,** and **V** in the two samples shown here.)

These Square capitals are written versions of Roman inscriptional letters, and Codex Sangallensis follows closely the forms, proportions and details of those carved classical capitals. Many changes of pen angle are required for this script. Overall, the pen angle is 'natural' (i.e. a right-handed scribe using a square-cut pen in a comfortable, slanted position), which gives the 'tilt' to the strokes of O and other rounded letters. Steeper pen angles are needed for certain diagonal and curved strokes (eg. the middle stroke of **S**). Upright strokes in **N** are not so fine as those in the Augusteus. Note the liberal use of pen manipulation and the corner of the pen in the formation of the serifs. The interlinear space is equal to the letter height, excepting the tall **F** and **L**. Indeed, the line ruling is practically identical to that of the Augusteus.

Codex Sinaiticus. London, British Library, Add. Ms. 43725 (Bible in Greek, the Old Testament mutilated, the New Testament complete). Also, *Codex Friderico-Augustanus,* Leipzig, Universitätsbibliothek (part of the Old Testament). This is one of the oldest surviving Greek vellum codices, *c.* AD 350. The place of writing is unknown, but it could well have been Alexandria or Caesarea.

The page size is now *c.* 14½" x 12¾" (370 x 325 mm). Generally, there are 48 lines in each of the four columns of text. Some 390 folios remain; originally, there were probably as many as 730. Of the Old Testament, 199 folios are in London and 43 are in Leipzig. The 148 folios of the New Testament are in London. The whole-page reproduction is taken from folio 7v, and the enlargement (four times actual size) from folio 245R which shows part of Luke 22: 63–64.

This manuscript was discovered in 1844 by the German scholar, Constantine Tishchendorf, in St Catherine's Monastery on Mount Sinai. He was allowed to take some of the leaves to Leipzig and, after a second visit in 1859, the rest was presented to the Tsar of Russia. The British Museum bought the Codex Sinaiticus in 1933.

There are two other surviving Greek Uncial Bibles written on vellum. Codex Vaticanus (Vatican, Ms. Gr. 1209) was perhaps written slightly earlier than Codex Sinaiticus. It used a three-column layout. Its script has the blunt monoline form and wide letter spacing, characteristic of the earliest Greek inscriptions (see *A1*). Maunde Thompson believed the manuscript was retouched, perhaps in the 10th century.

Codex Alexandrinus (London, British Library, Royal Ms. I. D. v–viii) was probably written early in the 5th century. Its pages have just two columns of text. The script is heavier and slightly wider than the other two, and it has more

developed serifs. Unlike the others, it uses larger, marginal initials at paragraph beginnings, and decorative panels to mark the end of certain Biblical books.

Codex Sinaiticus normally uses eight narrow columns per double-page spread, in imitation of the appearance of the earlier papyrus books in roll form. However, the Poetic books of the Old Testament are divided into verses, and arranged in two wide columns per page.

This manuscript was written by three scribes, recognized not so much by variations in their scripts, as by their differing abilities in spelling! Their errors are apparently very consistent, and yet so often phonetic, that many scholars believe this indicates that the manuscript was copied by means of dictation. The codex is heavily corrected. Tischendorf noted nearly 15,000 amendments in the London folios alone.

The freely-flowing Uncials of the Codex Sinaiticus, though written with a square-edged pen, took their general form and proportions from early monoline Greek inscriptions. But their penmanship was derived from cursive and semi-formal scripts to be seen on papyrus fragments dating from as early as the 4th century BC.

The narrow columns, the close interlinear space and the wide margins all heighten the textural quality of the writing. The script is largely unserifed and written rapidly. Note the characteristically flattened pen angle (possibly written more comfortably with a 'right oblique' pen or quill). This is maintained throughout except for occasional diagonal strokes of N and X. The letter C is the archaic form of sigma.

SIMILITERINAEGYPTO ETINALEXANDRIA
APUDCYRENEMQUOQ· ETTHEBAIDEM
MAGNASEDITIONECONTENDUNTUERUM
GENTILIUMPARSSUPERATINALEXANDRIA

XIIII IUDAEISMESOPOTAMIAREBELLANTIBUS
PRAECIPITIMPERATORTRAIANUSLYSIAEQTO
UTEOSPROUINCIAEXTERMINARETADUER
SUMQUOSQ·UETUSACIEMINSTRUENS
INFINITAMILIAEORUMINTERFICITETOB
HOCPROCURATORIUDAEAEABIMPERATO
REDECERNITUR

XIIII SALAMINAMURBEMCYPRIINTERFECTIS
INEAGENTILIBUSSUBUERTEREIUDAEI
TRAIANUSMORBOINSELENUNTIPERITSI
UETALIBISCRIPTUMLEGIMUSAPUDSE
LEUCIAMISAURIAEPROFLUUIOUENTRIS
EXTINCTUSESTANAETATISLXIIIMENS·IIII
DIESIIIIOSSAEIUSINURNAAUREAMCOL
LATAMETINFOROSUBCOLUMNATAPOSITA
SOLUSQUEOMNIUMINTRAURBEMSEPULT

CCXXIIIIOLYMP·
ROMANORUM XII REGNAUIT
HADRIANUS ANXXI

I HADRIANUSITALICAEINSPANIANATUSCO
SOBRINAETRAIANIFILIUSFUIT
HADRIANUSALEXANDRIAMAROMANIS
SUBUERSAMPUBLICISINSTAURAUITEXPENSIS
HADRIANUSTRAIANIINUIDENSGLORIAM
DEASSYRIAMESOPOTAMIAARMENIAQUAS
ILLEPROUINCIASFECERATREUOCAUITEXERCITUM

Marginal notes (right):

iudaeimultis / locisrebellant

unde

Traianusapud / seleuciamisau / riaeprofluuio / uentrisextin / ctusestet / ossaeiussubco / lumnaeiusin / forosepulta / suntquisolus / intraurbem / positusest

hadrianusgloria / traianiinuidens / deassyriamesopo / tamiaarmeniaex / ercitumreuo / cauit

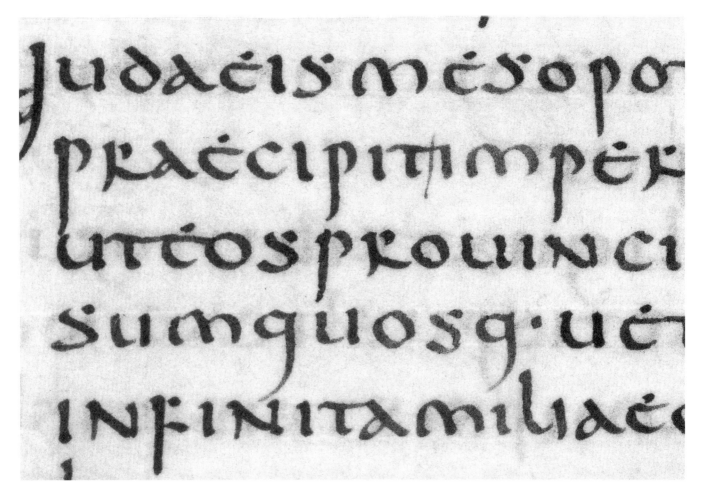

Oxford, Bodleian Library, Ms. Auct. T. 2. 26 (The *Chronicle* of Eusebius in Jerome's Latin version). Written in Italy, in the middle of the 5th century AD (the latest entry concerns events which happened in the year 444).

The page size is 8¾" x 6¾" (220 x 172 mm). The manuscript has 178 folios. Only folios 33R–145V are written in the 5th-century Uncial. The whole-page reproduction (actual size) and the enlargement (four times actual size) are both taken from folio 121R. Many folios have marginal and interlinear notes contemporary with the main text, written in a small 'sloping Uncial' style.

Most of the earliest surviving Uncial manuscripts have their origins in northern Africa: the oldest datable Uncial manuscript, for example, is from Hippo (St Petersburg, Public Library, Ms. Q. V. 1. 3) and was written AD 396–426 (see CLA 11: 1613 and Supplement page ix).

It has been suggested that the Uncial script was deliberately devised, at the time when Constantine was Emperor (AD 306–337), as a specifically Christian bookhand to replace the Square and Rustic capitals used for 'pagan' classics. However, there are some ancient scripts and inscriptions with certain Uncial characteristics, which clearly pre-date the time of Constantine (see Introduction, *Fig. 2*). The Timgad inscription of the 2nd or 3rd century, also has letters which are very similar to Uncial forms (see Stanley Morison, *Politics and Script,* page 63).

Furthermore, the existence of some early Christian texts written in *Rustics,* like the fragment of the Gospel of John (Aberdeen, University Library, Papyrus 2a) and the Epistle to the Ephesians (Florence, Ms. Laur. P. S. 1. 1306), as well as at least one 'pagan' author, Cicero, written in the 4th century in *Uncials* (Vatican, Ms. Lat. 5757), cast doubt on this common assertion.

The Chronicle is written in the early Italian style of Uncial (note the 'broken' character of **B**, **E**, **R** and **S**). It is an expert hand, rapidly written, with a substantially consistent 'natural', slanted pen angle (ie. a right-handed scribe using a square-cut pen in a comfortable position). There are few word divisions.

Note the inconsistencies to be expected in a tiny, quickly-written script. Look for the best examples of individual letters, eg. the **M** in the middle of line 5 (opposite) rather than the one in line 1. Note the change to a steeper pen angle for the upright strokes of **N**, and also its construction, revealed by the misaligned strokes of the second **N** in line 5 (above). The letter **O** could be more consistently round – there is a tendency for it to be rather pointed and small. Note also the typical Uncial 'ascenders' (**D**, **H**, **K** and **L**) and 'descenders' (**F**, **G**, **P**, **Q** and **Y**).

di filius et hominis fili
um est professus et
mortuum · amen

hilari epis lib x exp

inc eiusdem lib xi

Totum adqsolutum
fidae euangelicae sa
cramentum multifa
ria apostolus tractans
haecquoq inter cete
ra diuinae cognitionis
praecepta ad efesios
est locutus · sicut et
uos uocati estis in u
nas pe uocationis ues
trae unus dns una fi
des unum baptismu
unus ds et pater om
nium et per omnes
et in omnib · nobis
Non enim ambiguis nd
et erraticis indefini

tae doctrinae studi
is de reliquo uel ince
rtis opinionib incerta
humana permisit
statutis per sect op po
sitis obicib libertate
intellecentiae uolu
tatisq concludens
ut sapere non nisi ad
id tantum quod prae
dicatum a se fuerat
sincere cum perdeh
nitam fidei indemu
tabilis constitutio
nem credi aliterad
q aliter non liceret
(Nunc itaq · nobis dnm
praedicans unam fi
dem memorat de in
deu nilis dni unam
fidem memorans
unum etiam baptis
mum demonstrat
ut cum unius dni u
na fides esset unis
per hoc id dei in dni
unum unum esse
et baptismum et quia

Paris, Bibliothèque Nationale, Ms. Lat. 2630 (Hilarius *De Trinitate).* Written in Italy in the 5th or 6th century AD.

The page size is 10¾" x 9¼" (275 x 235 mm). The manuscript has 357 folios, including two (fols. 1 and 8) which are restorations of the *De Trinitate* text, apparently made at St Denis *c.* AD 800. Folios 356 and 357 contain a 7th-century fragment of the Book of Kings, and several other later additions are to be found in the main text. The whole-page reproduction and the enlargement (three times actual size) are both taken from folio 263v. The colophon in the left-hand column, written in red and black, marks the end of Hilary's Book 10 and the beginning of Book 11.

Early forms of Uncials, like this and the previous one *(B6),* evolved from scripts like that of the fragment of *De Bellis Macedonicis* (Introduction, *Fig. 2).* Although it was possibly written as early as AD 100, *De Bellis* has certain letterforms which have unmistakable Uncial character. And, most significantly, it used a slanted pen angle which was copied by all the early Uncial scripts. By contrast, early Half-uncial scripts used a flattened pen angle (see *C1).*

The meaning of the term 'Uncial' is obscure. Jerome is said to have been the first to speak of 'litterae uncialibis', a phrase which has perhaps been too literally translated as 'inch-high letters'. No ancient example of Uncial, used as text, nor any other early book script, comes anywhere *near*

that size. Bischoff *(Latin Palaeography, Antiquity and the Middle Ages)* believes that Mabillon (a 17th-century scholar) mistakenly applied Jerome's 'uncialibis' to this one style of script, and the error has been perpetuated ever since. Leonard Boyle *(Medieval Latin Palaeography)* suggests that 'uncialibis' is perhaps a mistranslation of 'initialibis'.

This manuscript, Lat. 2630, has a strong and vigorous Uncial script, written quickly yet very evenly spaced. It used a consistently 'natural' or slanted pen angle, simple forms of serifs (eg. on **C** and **S**), and has rather short descenders. The interlinear space is identical to its letter height. Its letterforms are satisfyingly round (see especially **C, D, G, H, M, O, Q** and **U**). Pen rotation is evident in the formation of some curved strokes.

Note the **A** with pointed bow, reminiscent of the Greek Uncial form *(B5);* the **E** which is often 'closed'; the hairline tail on **G**; the steeper pen angle needed for the vertical strokes of **N**, and the small bowl on **P**. Perhaps **F** and, occasionally, **L** are rather too slight; **S** is sometimes a little narrow and top-heavy; and the crossbar on **T** is short and uneven.

35

hic est panis decaelo discendens
ut siquis ex ipso manducauerit
NON MORIATUR

Ego sum panis uiuus
qui decaelo descendi
Siquis manducauerit ex hoc
pane uiuet in aeternum
et panis quem ego dabo
caro mea est pro mundi uita
Liticabant ergo iudaei
ad inuicem dicentes
Quomodo potest hic carnem
suam nobis dare
ad manducandum
dixit ergo eis ihs
Amen amen dico uobis
nisi manducaueritis carnem
filii hominis
et biberitis eius sanguinem

non habebitis uitam in uobis
Qui manducat meam carnem
et bibet meum sanguinem
habet uitam aeternam
et ego resuscitabo eum
in nouissimo die
Caro enim mea uere est cibus
et sanguis meus uere est potus
Qui manducat meam carnem
et bibit meum sanguinem
in me manet et ego in illo
Sicut misit me uiuens pater
et ego uiuo propter patrem
et qui manducat me
et ipse uiuet propter me
hic est panis qui decaelo discendit
non sicut manducauerunt
patres uestri manna
et mortui sunt

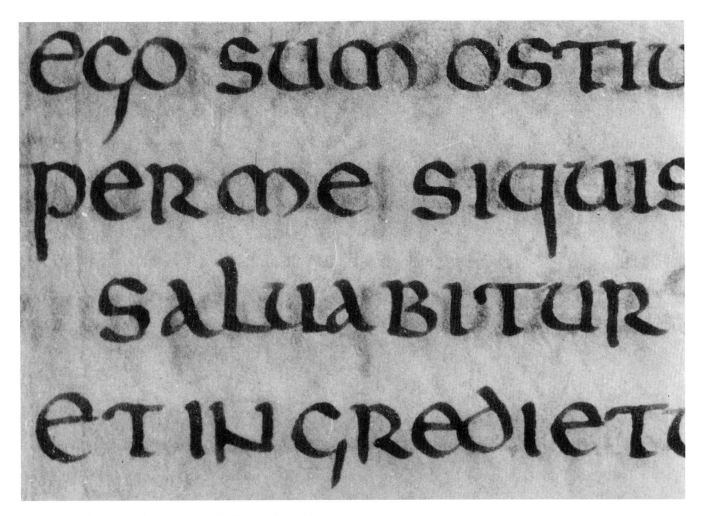

The St Cuthbert (Stonyhurst) Gospel. Blackburn, Stonyhurst College Library (the Gospel of John in Latin). The manuscript is currently exhibited in the British Library (Loan Ms. 74). Written by a scribe of the Wearmouth-Jarrow monasteries, probably *c.* AD 698. The manuscript was found in the tomb of St Cuthbert in 1104, hence its ascription.

The page size is 5¼" x 3⅝" (137 x 92 mm). The manuscript has 90 folios. The double-page spread reproduction (actual size) is taken from folio 28v–29R, and the enlargement (six times actual size) is from folio 46v. The spread (opposite) shows verses 50–58 of the Gospel of John, chapter 6.

Christianity and the Latin script were known in Britain from as early as the early 5th century AD. Augustine's evangelizing missions of AD 597 and 609 brought the Uncial script from Rome to Britain. Interestingly, no Irish manuscript is written in Uncials – the Roman missions never reached Ireland.

The twin Christian communities of Wearmouth-Jarrow in north-eastern England were founded in AD 674 and 681 by Benedict Biscop. He often visited Rome and brought back manuscripts, relics and works of art for the monasteries. The Wearmouth-Jarrow scribes developed their own expert copy of the Roman Uncial script. During the abbacy of Ceolfrith (689–716), they made three Great Bibles, one as a gift for the Pope and one for each of the monasteries.

This first one, Codex Amiatinus, is now in the Biblioteca Medicea-Laurenziana, Florence. Only fragments of the other Ceolfrith Bibles remain (London, British Library, Add. Ms. 37777, one leaf, and Add. Ms. 45025, eleven leaves). A further leaf, discovered in 1982 at Kingston Lacy House in Dorset, is also now in the British Library (Loan Ms. 81).

Whereas the text of the three Bibles was written in a style of Uncial called 'Roman' or 'artificial' (see *B10* notes), the St Cuthbert Gospel uses the less formal Uncial script which E A Lowe, the paleographer, refers to as 'capitular' (ie. that used in the Ceolfrith Bibles solely for chapter headings and colophons).

This tiny script is also an Anglo-Saxon version of earlier Italian Uncials. Compare it with *B7*, and note the similar **E**, **S** and **U**, and the different **A**, **M**, **N**, **P** and **T**. It was written quickly, with the 'natural' pen angle maintained. Because of the miniature format there are irregularities in the script, eg. the **O** is often less than round. Nevertheless, it shows a remarkable evenness and flow – despite the fact that it was certainly never intended as an exemplar.

CTINTCRROCAUITCOS
quoTpANesHABeTIS
quIdIxeRUNTSepTem
CTpRAeCepITTURBAe
DISCUMBeRescesupeR
TeRRAM
CTACCIpIeNSSepTem
pANes
CRATIASACeNS
fReCITCTdABATdISCI
pulISSUISUT
AppONeReNT
CTAppOSUERUNTTURBAe
eTHABeBANTpISCICU
LOSpAUCOS
CTIpSOSBeNedIXIT
CTIUSSITAppONI
CTMANdUCAUERUNT
CTSATURATISUNT
CTSUSTULERUNTquod
SUpeRAUeRAT
deFRACMeNTIS
SepTeMSpORTAS
CRANTAUTeMquIMAN
dUCAUeRUNT

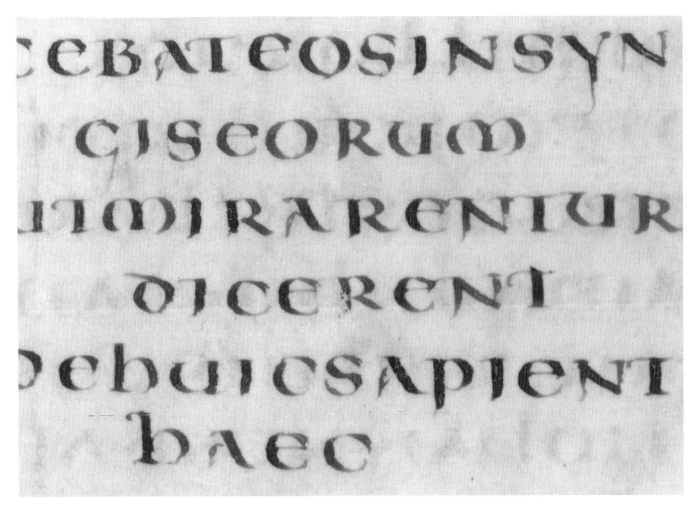

London, British Library, Harley Ms. 1775 (the Four Gospels in Latin). Written in Italy in the 6th century AD.

The page size is 7" x 4¾" (177 x 120 mm). The manuscript has 468 folios. The whole-page reproduction (actual size) is taken from folio 177v, and the enlargement (four times actual size) from folio 69R.

This is a small but elegantly-designed manuscript. The careful Uncial script is widely letter-spaced, but is without word divisions. The text is arranged with good interlinear spaces, in long and short lines largely following the sense of the words. The margins are generous and, originally, were probably even more striking.

The vellum is very thin, and on many folios there is a lot of 'show-through' from the reverse, despite the rather pale ink. On some pages it is almost orange (see Michael Gullick, *Calligraphy,* plate 3, colour reproduction). The corrections are made in a darker ink. The only decorative features in this manuscript are the first lines of each Gospel, which are written in red; the colophons, in alternating red and 'black'; and the enlarged, marginal initials written in Uncials, built-up with double strokes of the pen.

In this script we can see the forms of Uncial letters in transition. Early Uncials were written quickly, with a 'natural', slanted pen angle. Their letterforms were constructed simply, especially their serifs and other stem endings. Later

Uncials, dubbed 'artificial' by E A Lowe (see *B10* notes), were written much more deliberately, with a distinctly flatter pen angle. Their letter formation was much more complicated, especially their delicate, triangular serifs, which required the use of pen manipulation. Although the script of Harley 1775 has the appearance of a simple, early Uncial, some of its features betray a move towards a more sophisticated style. It has the much flatter pen angle and more deliberate letter formation of later Uncials, and its serifs are often made with pen twisting. Compare the triangular, sometimes 'forked', serifs of **C**, **E** and **S** in this manuscript with the same letters in *B7*.

Note the frequent use of the corner of the pen used for the decorative bow of **A**, and the long, hairline tails of **G**, **X** and **Y**. The triangular, 'forked' serif is also used on **L** and occasionally on **T** (see the end of lines 16 and 18). The flatter pen angle is apparent in many curved letters, and in the thin crossbars of **E** and **T**.

VERUMTAMEN DO SUBDITA ERIT ANIMA MEA

QUAM ABIPSO EST PATIENTIAM EA

ETENIM IPSE EST DS MEUS ET SALUTARIS MEUS

ADIUTOR MEUS NON EMIGRABO

IN DO SALUTARI MEO ET GLORIA MEA DS AUXILII

MEI SPES MEA IN DO EST

SPERATE IN EUM OMNIS CONUENTUS PLEBIS

EFFUNDITE CORAM ILLO CORDA UESTRA QUIA DS

ADIUTOR NOSTER EST

UERUMTAMEN UANI FILII HOMINUM MENDACES

FILII HOMINUM IN STATERIS UT DECIPIANT IP

SI DE UANITATE IN IDIPSUM

NOLITE SPERARE IN INIQUITATE ET IN RAPINIS

NOLITE CONCUPISCERE

DIUITIAE SI AFFLUANT NOLITE COR ADPONERE

SEMEL LOCUTUS EST DS DUO HAEC AUDIUI

QUIA POTESTAS DI EST ET TIBI DNE MISERICORDIA

QUIA TU REDDES SINGULIS SECUNDU OPERA

LXI PSALM DD CUM ESSET IN DESERTO IDUMEORU

DS MEUS AD TE DE LUCE UIGILO MEAE

SITIUIT IN TE ANIMA MEA QUAM MULTI

PLICITER ET CARO MEA

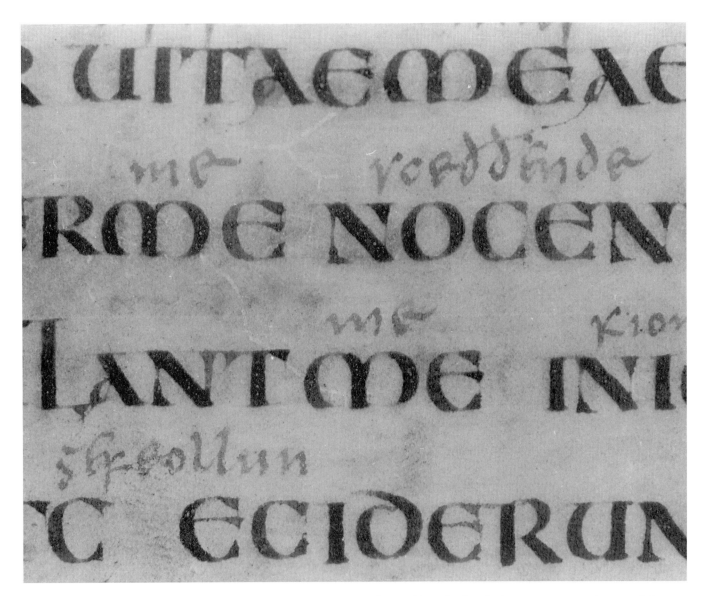

The Vespasian Psalter. London, British Library, Cotton Ms. Vespasian. A. i (Psalter with canticles). Written in southern England, most probably at St Augustine's, Canterbury, sometime between AD 725 and 750. The Mercian interlinear gloss was added a century later.

The page size is 9¼" x 7⅛" (235 x 180 mm). The manuscript has 153 folios. The whole-page reproduction is taken from folio 59R (part of Psalm 62 and 63), and the enlargement (five times actual size) from folio 31R (part of Psalm 27).

The monastery of St Augustine, Canterbury, was founded by missionaries from Rome. Its library contained Italian books from which English scribes undoubtedly copied.

This majestic Uncial script (which E A Lowe, the palaeographer, called 'artificial', presumably because of its complex letter construction, and Professor Julian Brown, following Armando Petrucci, called 'Roman', indicating its origin) is similar to, but not the same as, the Wearmouth-Jarrow Uncial used for the Codex Amiatinus (see *B8* notes). Despite the tiny writing of the Vespasian – its letters are only a fraction over ⅛" (3.5 mm) high – it compares very

favourably indeed with the more renowned script of the Wearmouth-Jarrow Bibles. Even at such a small scale, it combines sound construction with an immense amount of detail. The letter spacing is close but rhythmic, and there is a consistent use of word spaces.

Note the generally flattened pen angle (possibly written more comfortably with a 'right oblique' pen), and also the extensive use of pen manipulation in the formation of serifs, stem endings and rounded strokes. These are typical of the fully developed, 'artificial' form of Uncial. The corner of the pen must have been used for parts of **A** and **X**. Note also the marginal initials **D**, **N** and **V** etc. which, although pre-Carolingian, are built-up, compound letters derived from Roman inscriptional forms and Uncials. The title is written in the 'Vaticanus' *(B1)* style of Rustic capitals. The page layout is well-considered, and the interlinear space (double the letter height) emphasizes the grandeur of this precisely-written script.

obliuisci profecto interrogationis tuae
mea responsio defuisset

EXP EPISTULA · SANCTI AUGUSTINI DE

CURA PRO MORTUIS GERENDA

INCP EIUSDEM LIB · ENCHIRIDION

Codex Bambergensis. Bamberg, Staatsbibliothek, Ms. Patr. 87 (B. iv. 21) (Works of Jerome and Augustine). Written in southern Italy, probably near Naples, during the 6th century AD.

The page size is 11½" x 8½" (293 x 215 mm). The manuscript has 138 folios. The whole-page reproduction and the enlargement (three and a half times actual size) are both taken from folio 95R, part of Augustine's *Enchiridion*.

When the term 'Half-uncials' was first used it was probably thought that such scripts were a degenerate form of Uncials. In fact, despite similarities seen in certain late examples (see Introduction, *Fig. 5*), they were not directly derived from Uncials at all. Early Uncials developed from scripts like the *De Bellis* (see Introduction, *Fig. 2)* and retained a 'natural' (slanted) pen angle. Early Half-uncials, however, developed from scripts such as that of the Livy *Epitome* fragments (see Introduction, *Fig. 1)*, and their evolution was characterised by the use of the flattened pen angle, as were the early Greek scripts (cf. *B5*). The 'clubbed' ascenders seen in this Bamberg manuscript indicate an additional source, New Roman cursive, which employs looped ascenders to facilitate ligatures, (see Introduction, *Fig. 4)*.

Many Half-uncial scripts betray, all too obviously, their transitional nature (uncertain letter structures and some incompatible letterforms) and this diminishes their useful-

ness as models. This Bamberg manuscript, while not without faults (it was written very rapidly and the letters are small), is perhaps the most confident of the Half-uncial examples surviving. It incorporates a nicely formed Uncial and some fine Square capitals (see Introduction, *Fig. 8*).

Overall the pen angle is consistently flat, perhaps just 5° or 10° from the writing line. It is a little steeper for letters like the flourished **x**, and for some finishing strokes. Note the surprisingly full tail of the **g** (a letter reminiscent of a figure 5) and the low sweep of the branch of the **r**. The letter **d** (and to a lesser degree, **b**, **p**, and **q**) has an unusual form, being made like a complete letter o with an upright stroke added. This is not a feature of Carolingian scripts (cf. *C5* and *C6*), but it does reoccur in manuscripts of the 11th and 12th centuries (see especially *C8,* but also *C9* and *D1)*, and also in many of the minuscule hands of the Renaissance (cf. *F3, F4, F5,* and *F11)*. The bulbous ascenders, because they derive from the loops of an earlier cursive hand, would undoubtedly be made by first pushing the pen upwards and then, without lifting, moving over and down to complete the vertical strokes. See also *C7* notes.

ab hominib:

amen dico uobis

receperunt

mercedem suam

te autem faciente

aelemosyna nesciat

sinistra tua quid

faciat dextera tua

ut sit elemosyna tua

in abscondito

et pater tuus qui uidet

in abscondito

reddet tibi

et cum oratis non eritis

sicut hypocritae

qui amant in synagoga

togis ...

platearum

stantes orare

ut uideantur

ab hominib:

amen dico uobis

receperunt

mercedem suam

tu autem cum oradis

intra in cubiculum tuum

et clauso ostio tuo ora

patrem tuum

in abscondito

et pater tuus qui uidet

in abscondito

reddet tibi

orantes autem

nolite multum loqui

sicut ethnici faciunt

putant enim qui

in multiloquio suo

exaudiantur

nolite ergo assimilari

scit enim pater uester

quid: opus sit uobis

antequam

petatis eum

sic ergo uos orabitis

Pater noster qui es

in caelis sanctificetur

nomen tuum

adueniat regnum tuum

The Lindisfarne Gospels. London, British Library, Cotton Ms. Nero D. iv (the Four Gospels complete, in the Latin Vulgate version, with Canon Tables, Gospel Introductions, Lists of Lessons, etc.). Written in north-eastern England at Lindisfarne, *c.* AD 698.

The page size is 13⅜" x 9½" (340 x 235 mm). The manuscript has 259 folios. The whole-page reproduction is from folio 37R, showing part of the Gospel of Matthew and the enlargement (three times actual size) is from folio 18V, part of the Introduction to that Gospel.

The interlinear Anglo-Saxon gloss (the earliest surviving English translation of the Gospels) was added *c.* AD 950 by Aldred (calling himself 'an unworthy and most miserable priest') who also glossed Ms. Bodl. 819 *(C4)*. He says, in a note added to this Lindisfarne manuscript, that the original text was written by Eadfrith (Bishop of Lindisfarne, 698–721) and that the book was bound by Ethelwald, (Bishop from 724–740). This sumptuous ceremonial book, with its fifteen elaborately decorated pages and majestic script, testifies to the magnificence and beauty of Anglo-Saxon art.

Insular Half-uncial scripts were first used in Christian Ireland. Most probably they developed from Italian cursive Half-uncials like those of the 6th-century AD Arator manuscript offset (Oxford, Bodleian Library, e. Museo 66, see *CLA* Supplement 1740). One of the earliest known Irish manuscripts, Codex Usserianus (Dublin, Trinity College Ms. 55, see *CLA* 2: 271) written *c.* AD 600, shows a script which is somewhere between the Italian Half-uncial and the Insular.

The Insular Half-uncial was to spread to Anglo-Saxon Northumbria and become a speciality of northern Britain. Only later was it copied elsewhere, usually in places influenced by Celtic missionary activity. Two other scripts characteristic of Anglo-Saxon manuscripts were the Wearmouth-Jarrow Uncials (see the notes on *B8)* – which T J Brown suggested influenced the character of the Lindisfarne script – and Insular minuscules *(C4)*. The two-column layout of the Gospels also follows the Wearmouth-Jarrow pattern (these places being only 40 miles away from Lindisfarne).

Note the characteristic roundness of the letters, the flattened pen angle (possibly written more comfortably with a 'right oblique' pen), the wedge serif (probably done with the corner of the pen for **d**, **g** and **t**) and the alternative letterforms (eg. **a**, **d**, **n**, **r** and **s**). The beginnings of Italic-style branching can be seen in Aldred's minuscule gloss.

sanguihem iusum· Etilli dixerunt
quid adnos tu uideris· Et proiecis se
suspendit· Tunc prihapes sacerdo
tum acceptis argenteis dixerunt non
licet eos mittere incorban quia pre
tium sanguinis est· Consilio autem ini
to emerunt exillis agrum figuli inse
pulturam peregrinorum propter hoc
uocatus est ager ille acheldemach id
est ager sanguinis usque inhodiernum
diem· Tunc impletum est quod dictum
est perhieremiam prophetam dicentem
Et acceperunt triginta argenteos preti
um adpretiati quem adpretiauerunt
filii israhel & dederunt eos inagrum
figuli sicut constituit mihi dns̄ / Ihcer
Ihs autem stetit ante praesidem &
rogauit eum praeses dicens tu es
rex iudeorum dicit ei ihs̄ tu dicis· Et cum
accussaretur a principibus sacerdotum

clere sed pucius

corpus ecclina

nonne duo pass

ulius ecclus non

a *The Lichfield (St Chad) Gospels.* Lichfield, Cathedral Library (Three Gospels in Latin; the manuscript now ends at Luke 3:9). Written, possibly in Wales, between AD 710 and 720. The book is known to have been at Llandaff by the 8th century – some notes are written in 'Welsh minuscule'.

The page size is 12⅛" x 8¾" (308 x 223 mm). The manuscript has a total of 236 pages. The whole-page reproduction is taken from page 131, which shows part of Matthew, and the enlargement (twice actual size) is taken from page 43.

This is one of a few, magnificent Gospel Books to survive from the 7th and 8th centuries AD. It has eight fully-decorated pages, including three Evangelist portraits. The illumination was undoubtedly influenced by the artist of the Lindisfarne Gospels. On page 220 there is an extraordinarily elaborate Cross Carpet design, delicately coloured, which bears a striking resemblance to the better-known one from Lindisfarne.

The writing in the great Insular Gospel books varies. That of the Book of Durrow (Dublin, Trinity College Ms. 57, *c.* 680) is a little uncertain; in the Book of Kells (Dublin, Trinity College Ms. 58, *c.* 790–800) it is perhaps over precise; and in the Lindisfarne Gospels *(C2, c.* 698) it is rather heavy. However, the St Chad script (which has similarities with one of the hands in the Book of Kells) is rhythmic and lively, yet maintains firm structure. The line length is much longer than in the two-column layout of the Lindisfarne Gospels.

Note the typical roundness of the letter shapes and the flattened pen angle; the upright **d**; and the two forms of **n**.

b Oxford, Bodleian Library, Ms. Lat. d. 1 (P) (one leaf of the Gospel of John, once used as part of the binding of Dymock Parish Register, Gloucester). Written in England sometime during the 8th century AD; the marginal capitals were later retouched.

The overall size of the fragment is 10¾" x 8¾" (273 x 223 mm). The section shown is actual size.

This is an unusually lightweight script for Insular manuscripts, written with a delicate touch. Note the 'Uncial' forms of **A** and **B** in lines 2 and 4.

peregrinorum]

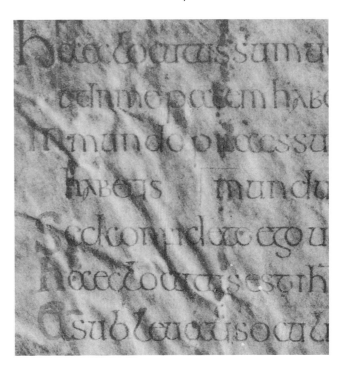

QUI DIMITTITUR UOLUNTATIS SUAE. CONFUNDET
MATREM SUAM; ~ de hac uirga apostolus ad corinthios.
an uultis inuirga ueniam uel uos: an in spu mansuetudinis:
puto nam que quam exequitur rime corripiendum & diuci
bilum ammonet populus di. qui si non assiduis monitis
& inspirationibus sacerdotum regitur castigatur congrega
tione gignat ecclesiae. detrahentibus his qui propius sint
religioni fidei xpianae; Unde recte subiungitur; ~
CUM PROPHETIA DEFECERIT. DISSIPABITUR
POPULUS: QUI CUSTODIT LEGEM. BEATUS EST;
quia nimirum cum defraudat sacerdotalis iudicio:
soluitur continuo disciplina diuinae legis: qua popu
lus ad beatitudinis praemia peruenire debuisset; ~
UIDISTI HOMINEM UELOCEM AD LOQUENDUM.
STULTI MAGIS SPERANDA EST QUAM ILLIUS
CORREPTIO; ~ Quare quidem initium stultitiae sed
non leuius + uerbositatis; nam saepe contingit ut hebes
aliqui & ipse rudis qui nescius litterarum atque uerba salu
tiferae correptionis accipiat. qui a is qui ex eruditia
fiditur sermonis magis sua quae nouit & quae nouit se
se autumat iactantia profiteri quam dicta sapienti
um audire concedit; ~

Oxford, Bodleian Library, Ms. Bodl. 819 (Bede's Commentary on the Book of Proverbs). Written at Wearmouth-Jarrow, the Venerable Bede's own monastery, in the second half of the 8th century AD.

The page size is 9¾" x 6⅞" (248 x 175 mm). The manuscript has 115 folios. The whole-page reproduction and the enlargement (three and a half times actual size) are both taken from folio 95R.

Aldred, who glossed the Lindisfarne Gospels *(C2),* also added interlinear notes to this manuscript, sometime before AD 971. The Biblical text is written in a very fine 'capitular' Uncial (see *B8),* and Bede's Commentary is written in a mature example of Anglo-Saxon minuscule.

This Insular minuscule is probably not a development from the formal Insular Half-uncial. It seems more likely that it is derived from examples of contemporary cursive handwriting, similar to the marginal notes in Bodleian Library, Ms. Douce 140, thought to be written by St Boniface *(CLA* 2: 237). It must be noted, however, that Boniface lived in southern England, and is unlikely to have influenced the scribes at Wearmouth-Jarrow.

This script is not as informal as it first appears. For example, **m**, **n**, **p**, long **r**, and long **s** are all generally made with two or three separate strokes. Note, however, the steep pen angle and the compressed letter shapes which contrast well with the flattened pen angle and the roundness of the Uncials. Note also the numerous ligatures, the open **a** and **d**, the tall **c** and **e** in ligature, and some archaic letterforms. The letters **p**, **r** and **s** are very similar. The first words of the minuscule script (opposite) read: 'de hac virga apostolus'.

INCP EPLA AD
HEBRAEOS

Cap. I. MVLTIFARIE MVL
TISQ; MODIS OLIM DS
LOQVENS PATRIBVS IN
PROPHETIS NOVISSIME
diebus istis locutus e nobis in filio
quem constituit heredem uniuersoru per que
fecit et saecula. Qui cum sit splendor gloriae
et figura substantiae eius. portansq; omnia
uerbo uirtutis suae. purgationem peccatoru
faciens. sedet ad dexteram maiestatis in excelsis.
tanto melior angelis effectus quanto differen
tius prae illis nomen hereditauit. Cui enim dixit
aliquando angelorum filius meus es tu. ego hodie
genuite? Et rursum ego ero illi in patre. et
ipse erit mihi in filium. Et cum iteru introducit
primogenitu in orbem terrae dicit. Et adorent
eum omnes angeli di. Et ad angelos quidem dicit
qui facit angelos suos sps. et ministros suos flam
mam ignis. Ad filium aut. Thronus tuus ds in
scm scli. Et uirga aequitatis uirga regni tui.
Dilexisti iustitiam et odisti iniquitate. prop
terea unxit te ds ds tuus. Oleo exultationis prae
participib; tuis. Et tu in principio dne terram
fundasti. et opera manuum tuarum sunt caeli.
Ipsi peribunt tu aut permanebis. Et omnes ut
uestamentum ueterescent. Et uelut amictum
mutabis eos et mutabuntur. Tu autem idem
ipse es. Et anni tui non deficient.

II. Ad quem autem angelorum dixit aliquando sede
a dextris meis quoadusq; ponam inimicos tuos
scabellum pedum tuorum? Nonne omnes sunt
amministratorii sps in ministerium missi prop

Cap. 2. ter eos qui hereditatem capient salutis? Prop
terea abundantius oportet obseruare nos ea
quae audiuimus ne forte per effluamus. Si eni
qui per angelos dictus e sermo factus e firmus
et omnis praeuaricatio et inoboedientia accepit
iustam mercedis retributionem quomodo nos ef
fugiemus si tantam neglexerimus salutem? Quae
cum initium accepisset enarrari per dnm ab eis
qui audierunt in nobis confirmata e. Contestan
te do signis et portentis et uariis uirtutib; et sps
sci distributionib; secundum suam uoluntatem.

IIII. Non enim angelis subiecit ds orbem terrae futuru
de quo loquimur. testatus e aut in quodam loco

quis dicens. Quid est homo quod memor es eius.
aut filius hominis qnm uisitas eum? Minuisti
eu paulo minus ab angelis. gloria et honore
coronasti eu. Et constituisti eu super opera ma
nuum tuaru. Omnia subiecisti sub pedibus eius.
In eo eni quod omnia subiecit. nihil dimisit non
subiectu ei. Nunc aut nec du uidemus omnia
subiecta ei. Cum aut qui modico quam angeli
minoratus e. Uidemus ihm propter passione
mortis gloria et honore coronatu ut gratia
di pro omnib; gustaret morte. Decebat enim
eum propter quem omnia et per quem omnia
qui multos filios in gloria adduxerat auctore
salutis eoru per passiones consummare. Qui eni
scificat et qui scificantur ex uno omnes.

IIII. Propter quam causam non confunditur fratres
eos uocare dicens. nuntiabo nomen tuu fratrib;
meis in medio ecclesiae laudabo te. Et iterum
Ego ero fidens in eum. Et iteru. Ecce ego et pueri
mei quos mihi dedit ds. Quia ergo pueri comu
nicauerunt carni et sanguini et ipse similiter par
ticipauit eisdem. ut per mortem destrueret eu
qui habebat mortis imperiu id est diabolum. ut
liberaret eos qui timore mortis per totam uita
obnoxii erant seruituti. Nusquam eni angelos
apprehendit. Unde debuit per omnia fratrib;
similare. ut misericors fieret et fidelis ponti
fex ad dm. Ut repropriaret delicta populi
in eo enim in quo passus e ipse temptatus po
tens e. Et eis qui temptantur auxiliari.

Cap. 3. Vnde fratres sci uocationis caelestis participes
Considerate apostolu et pontificem confessionis
nrae ihm qui fidelis e ei qui fecit illu sicut et
moyses in omni domo illius. Amplioris eni gloriae
iste prae moyse dignus habitus e. Quantoam
pliorem honorem habet domus qui fabricauit
illa. Omnis namq; domus fabricatur ab aliquo.
Qui aut omnia creauit ds e. Et moyses quide
fidelis erat in tota domo eius tanqua famulus
in testimonium eoru quae dicenda erat. Xps
uero tanqua filius in domo sua. Quae domus
sumus nos si fiducia et gloria spei usq; ad finem fir
mum retineamus. Quapropter sicut dicit sps
scs. hodie si uocem eius audieritis. nolite obdurare
corda ura. sicut in exacerbatione secundu diem
temptationis in deserto. Ubi temptauerunt me
patres uri. probauerunt et uiderunt opera mea
quadraginta annis. propter quod infensus fui
generationi huic et dixi semper errant corde
ipsi autem non cognouerunt uias meas sicut iuraui

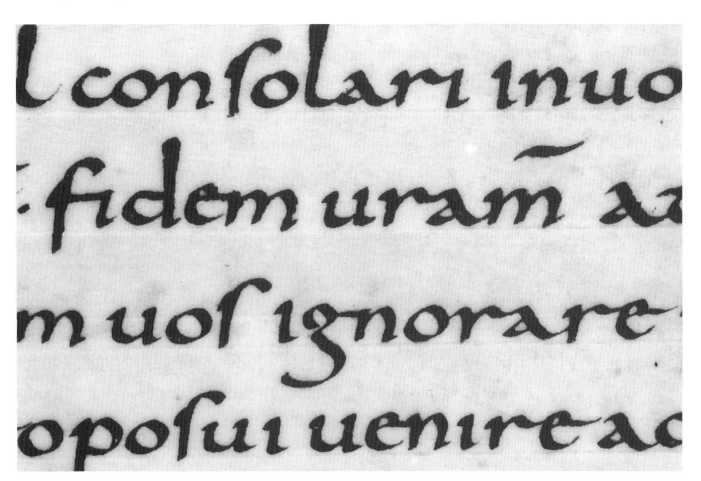

The Moutier Grandval Bible. London, British Library, Add. Ms. 10546 (Latin Vulgate Bible in one volume). Written at St Martin's Abbey, Tours in France during the abbacy of Adalhard, AD 834–843.

The page size is 19¾" x 14½" (500 x 370 mm). The manuscript has 449 folios. The whole-page reproduction is taken from folio 438v, and shows the opening chapters of the Epistle to the Hebrews. The enlargement (four times actual size) is from folio 411v, part of Romans 1: 12–13.

Nearly 100 Bibles were produced by the scriptorium at Tours in the years AD 800–850, in addition to many other liturgical and classical texts. Many of these, in whole or in part, have survived. David Ganz (1994) lists eighteen Bibles and thirteen fragments known to exist. Two others of similar size and quality to the Moutier Grandval are CLM. 12741 now in Munich (see *E1*), written *c.* AD 830, and one in Paris (Ms. Lat. 1) written during the abbacy of Vivian in AD 843.

The large format, the generous margins, and the richness of decoration reveal the prestigious nature of these manuscripts. The hierachy of scripts – a large initial, Versal capitals, Uncials and minuscules (in descending order) – are used to great effect.

The emergence of the Caroline minuscule is one of the great developments in the history of calligraphy. It derived from ancient Roman Half-uncial scripts (like *C1*), incorporating features from local hands. The abbey of Corbie played a major rôle in its evolution, especially with its Maudramnus script (see Ganz, 1987 and Knight, *Scripts of the Grandval Bible,* 1990). It is a mature script of enduring quality. It was to be copied and adapted in succeeding centuries by scribes in England, Germany and Italy. Humanist scribes revived it, early in the 15th century, as an appropriate hand for the copying of classical texts (see *F3–F5).* The first Italian printers then adopted it, and it has remained the basis of Western typography to this day.

The script of the Moutier Grandval Bible, though very small, is extremely consistent and well formed. Even some of the larger scripts of the Gospels and Psalters made at Tours (eg. British Library Harley Mss. 2790 and 2793) lack its rhythm and structure.

The cursive character of the script is encouraged by the size and speed at which it was written. It can be discerned in the slight forward slope, the wideness of such letters as **a, d, m, n, q** and **u,** and the 'branching' character of **m, n** and **r** (usually written without pen lifts). The angle of the pen is quite flat, about 25° to the base line. Note the forms of **a, f, g,** long **s** and **t,** so typical of mature Caroline minuscules, and the tall ascenders with their heavily-wedged serifs. The lines of text are separated by very wide interlinear spaces.

Concupiui salutare tuum dñe ·
& lex tua meditatio mea est ·
Viuet anima mea & laudabit te ·
& iudicia tua adiuuabunt me ·
Erraui sicut ouis quę periit ·
quaere seruum tuum dñe
quia mandata tua ñ sū oblitus ·

CANTICUM GRADUUM ·

d dñm cum tribularer ·
clamaui & exaudiuit me ·
dñe libera animā meā ·
a labiis iniquis
& a lingua dolosa ·
quid detur tibi aut quid apponat
tibi · ad linguam dolosam ·
sagittae potentis acutae
cum carbonibus desolatoriis ·
heu mihi quia incolatus meus

eum in secula

angeli dni dno.

aquae omis quae

r dno. b omfui

The Ramsey Psalter. London, British Library, Harley Ms. 2904 (Latin Psalter with canticles). Written in southern England, probably in the Cathedral Priory at Winchester for use at Ramsey Abbey, *c.* AD 974–986. The text is divided according to a pattern established at Winchester. The scribe of this Psalter has also been linked with a manuscript in Cambridge, Sidney Sussex College, Ms. 100 (part ii).

The page size is 13" x 9¾" (330 x 250 mm), with letters approximately ⅕" (5 mm) high. The manuscript has 214 folios. The whole-page reproduction is taken from folio 164R (showing Psalm 120), and the enlargement (two and a half times actual size) from folio 201V (part of the Benedicite).

There are a number of English manuscripts written in a version of Caroline minuscule, but none so distinctive or so imposing as this. Edward Johnston, in his first book, recognized that 'this extremely legible MS would form an almost perfect model for a modern formal hand' *(Writing & Illuminating, & Lettering,* 1906), and he later used it as the basis for his 'Foundational' hand. Johnston used the term 'Foundational' not only because the hand makes an excellent starting point, but also because it is capable of much adaptation and development. 'I doubt if there is any other MS extant that would make so good a Strain from which to breed Varieties' (extract from a letter to Paul Standard, reproduced in *Formal Penmanship* as plate 13).

The liturgical purpose of the manuscript has influenced the size and character of this hand. What is possible and desirable on a large scale cannot be readily incorporated into a smaller script, and vice versa (see *C5*).

This powerful and assured hand is very soundly constructed and almost completely free of mannerisms. Note the round **o** (the outline of which is like two overlapping circles) and the other letters which take their form from it: **b, c, d, e, m, n, q, u.** Edward Johnston chose folio 201V as the clearest illustration of the fundamental structure of the **o** and its related letters. Note the vigorous arches of **m** and **n**, the wedge serifs, and the very slight forward stance. Note also the slightly uncertain form of **a**, the rather weak tail of **g**, the occasional use of an alternative **r**, the long **s**, and the upright **t** (in ligature). The curious use of **&** (lines 3 and 14) is perhaps peculiar to English scribes (see also *C7* and *C8*).

The heading is written in red Rustic capitals, and the initials are Versals, generally with 'Uncial' form. Elsewhere in the manuscript the scribe uses Rustics for the rather rare initial 'capitals'. Later, the Humanist scribes eventually adopted Square capitals for the same purpose.

carbonibus desolat

uirginem & martyrem adquisisti
fide honorasti pudore. glorifi
casti certamine · AMEN ·
Repleatur hic populus illo spú. qui
mar̄r̄i tuae affuit agathae. cum
eam ignis torreret. cum ungula
raderet. cum aculeus infigeret.
cum mamilla torqueret AMEN
Ut dum se sibi pro tuo amore abne
gat. tua collocetur indextera.
cuius est electione uocata inglo
riam · AMEN ·
Quod ipse praestare dignetur

INNL SCI UEDASTI. CONF

DS FUNDATOR FIDEI.
& indultor sacerdotii.
congregatio plebis. sci
ficatio confessoris. qui be
atum uedastum adhoc armasti.

The Benedictional of Aethelwold. London, British Library, Add. Ms. 49598 (Episcopal liturgical blessings). Written in southern England, at the Old Minster in Winchester, AD 971–984. A Latin poem at the beginning of the manuscript states that it was written for St Aethelwold who was Bishop of Winchester from AD 963–984, by the scribe Godeman. Godeman became Abbot of Thorney in Lincolnshire but was probably once a monk of the Old Minster. He also wrote part of a manuscript now at the College of Arms in London (Arundel Ms. 22, folios 84 and 85).

The page size is 11½" x 8½" (292 x 216 mm). The manuscript has 119 folios. The whole-page reproduction and the enlargement (three times actual size) are both taken from folio 36R.

This is another majestic version of the English Caroline minuscule, in a manuscript more renowned for the lavish illumination which befits its ceremonial purpose. The manuscript contains some outstanding Versal capitals (see *E3).* The page layout is similar to that of the Ramsey Psalter *(C6)* but the overall weight is much lighter. Another Benedictional from Winchester with identical content and very similar script to the Aethelwold manuscript is now in Paris (Bibliothèque Nationale, Ms. Lat. 987).

The script, while having a great deal of character, is not quite so ingenuous as that of the Ramsey Psalter. The scribe deviates quite frequently from the generally 'natural' pen angle, especially in the formation of **m**, **n** and **u**, where a certain rotation of the pen can be detected, and the writing has a distinct forward slant. The bulbous ascenders were not made with pen pressure, nor by double stroking. They were the result of the pushing stroke used in Roman Half-uncial scripts (see *C1* notes). The ascenders in other Caroline minuscule hands are made in a similar manner (compare those in *C5, C6* and *C8).* Even the Protogothic script from Canterbury *(D1)* retains the long-established practice.

Note the large bowl and weak tail of the **g**; the 'Uncial' form of **h**; the strange **ra** ligature (line 2, opposite), a feature noticeable in certain pre-Caroline scripts (see also *C8);* and the use of **&** within words (lines 6 and 7), also seen in *C6* and *C8.* Red Uncials are used for marginal initials, headings and 'amens'.

ente. quiuiuis. ALIA.

Suscipiat pietas tua dne dsmis humilitatis mee
preces. & pintercessiones & merita beate & glo
riose sempq; uirginis. & di genitricis mariae. om_
niumq; scoru tuorum. erue & libera me famulu
tuu .ill'. demanib: inimicorum meoru. & depo
testate satane. & ministrorum eius. ac decarnalib:
corporis mei desideriis. atq; deomnib: huius scli
uanitatib: libera me dne. quatinus te miserante
aeternorum flammas tormentorum euadere
ualeam. atq; adppetuam beatitudinem merear
puenire. Te auxiliante. quiuiuis.

OR DETRIBULATIONE TEMPTATIONUM.

Salua me dne rex aeterne gle. qui potes saluare.
& da mihi ghrm ut uelim operari & pficere
que tibi placeant. & mihi adsalute expediant.
One sce pat omps ds. da mihi intribulatione au_
xilium. inpsecutione solacium. & inomni tepore
teptationis uirtutem. One sce. & pie pat. da m
depreteritis peccatis ueniam. depresentib: emen_
dationem. ac defuturis adhibe mihi custodiam.
quia nullu malum dimittere possum. nec bonu
facere. nisisuccurrat mihi miscda tua magna

The Arundel Psalter. London, British Library, Arundel Ms. 155 (Psalter in Latin). Written in southern England by Eadvius Basan, scribe of Christ Church, Canterbury, between AD 1012 and 1023. The interlinear Anglo-Saxon gloss was added soon afterwards.

The page size is 11¾" x 8¼" (297 x 210 mm). The manuscript has 193 folios. The whole-page reproduction and the enlargement (three times actual size) are both taken from folio 182R.

Ten other manuscripts (or fragments) have been attributed to Eadvius Basan. They include the Eadui Codex in Hanover (Kestner-Museum, Hs. W. M. XXIa, 36), a Gospel (British Library, Add. Ms. 34890), the Cnut Charter of 1018 (British Library, Stowe Charter 38), some pages in the Harley Psalter (British Library, Harley Ms. 603, folios 28R–49V) and in the Vespasian Psalter (British Library, Cotton Ms. Vespasian A. i, Part ii, folios 155–160).

The beginnings of Gothic compression can be seen in this expert and beautiful script. Firm structure, rhythmic movement and lightness of weight are maintained but there is an insistent narrowness. The script has some similarities with the earlier English script of the Benedictional of

Aethelwold (see C7). The same rotation of the pen can be seen particularly in the arched strokes of **m** and **n**. At the outset the pen is quite steep, then it flattens, especially for the final serif stroke.

Note the wedge-shaped serifs (see C7 notes); the linked **ra** (eg. line 9), also seen in C7; and the use of **&** as part of words, also seen in C6 and C7. In line 14 a cedilla is added to **&** represent 'æt'. Note also the alternative **r** (eg. line 6); the upright form of **t** when ligatured (eg. line 7); and the curiously ligatured **rt** in 'virtutem' (line 19).

The construction of **b, d, p** and **q** is unusual. These letters seem to be made of a complete o shape with an upright stroke added. This feature occurs elsewhere (see C1 notes), but nowhere quite so distinctly as in the hand of Eadui.

The headings are written in Rustic capitals, and the large Versal initials are each three writing lines high.

offer munus tuū ·ad illū enī te hoc dictum nos ammonet ·omīs loquens ·
ut et nos dona et munera nr̄a non tene-
amus apud nos ·sed reddamus deo nostro ·maxime cū de aliqua liberamur
tribulatione ·Offer inquit munus tuū ·
Quare ·ut omīs qui uident te portare
et offerre ·credant hiis mirabilibȝ ·et magnificent dr̄m qui misertus est tui ·et in
fidelibȝ per hoc increpatio ·et testimonium duritie cordis ipsorū fiet ·Sic
et illū triginta et octo annis iacentē
in infirmitatem erigens a langore ·
iussit portare grabattū suū et ire in
domū suā ·ut hunc ipsum lectus porta-
tus ·a beo p mediā ciuitatē clamas-
set saluante se inuocando ·Sic et illū
cecū in natatoria syloe misit ·ut uiden-
tes eum ambulare illuc euntem cecū
et iterū remeantē mirati et obstupe-
scentes crederent ·huic talia mirabilia
facientī ·Post hec que superius dicta
sunt cū introisset capharnaū in ciuita-
tem galilee ·Si cognominata ē caphar-
naum inqua sepius dr̄s uirtutis sue
magnificentiā demonstrauit ·Ingre-
diente in eo capharnaū ·Capharnaū
namqȝ interpretatur ager ·uel uilla
consolationis ·Cum ager quod in eo
aliquid agatur ·uel uilla a circū uall-
atione limitis ·hoc ē munitione custo-
die nom̄ acceperint ·Congrua dispen-
satione carnis illo ingressus asseritur
dr̄s quo p deitatis potentiā circum
dando attrahens ad credulitatē incre-
dulos ·et sanitatis miraculū erat actu-
rus ·Accessit centurio exter generatio-
ne ·sed mente domesticus ·militum
princeps ·sed plus anglorū gaudium ·
Accessit ad eū centurio ·Increpatio hic
nempe illorū ostenditur ascendentiū
quondā a bello incarnelo quinqua-
genariorū qui manentes in fidelitate
celesti sunt igne consūpti ·iste uero ex
infideli particeps fidei factus ·in sinu
ilico deputatus ē abrahe ·Accessit ad
eum centurio rogans eū et dicens ·Dr̄ne
puer m̄s iacet in domo paraliticus et
male torquetur ·Multi illo tēpore

pro diuersis rogabant infirmitatibȝ ·nul-
lus tam̄ p seruo ·nisi iste solus ·Et hoc
ei x augmtū beatitudinis et coronā
glē erat ·Quid enī in mentis abdito di-
gnum uouens iudicii centurio iste age-
bat ·michi hic seruus ē et ego creatoris ·
iste me sup terrā ·et ego magnū in celis
habeo dr̄m ·Si ego ei ñ misereor quom
ille michi miserebitur ·Si ego huic ñ
subuenio ·quomodo michi ille subue-
niet ·Sic debent omīs qui famulos ha-
bent et famulas cogitare ·sic miserere
et condolere eis supplicare ·et curam
habere deseruis uel ancillis suis ·sicut
et ille beatus centurio fecit ·Puer m̄s
inquit iacet in domo ·Non in una rē
tantū miserabilis quod iacet ·sed in
alia quod paraliticus ·tertia quod male torquetur ·Omnia enī ista dolorē
cognominauit ·et iacentē paraliticū
et dure detentū ideo ut sue anime an-
gustias demonstraret ·et dr̄m cogno-
uisset quatenus illius cruciatū mon-
straret ·et dr̄m benuolentiā inuitaret ·
Puer m̄s iacet in domo ·Et huic quare
non attulisti eū ·ideo ait ·qa non opus
est illi ostendere omiā uidentī ·ñ opus
est in conspectu afferre eis ·cuius poten-
tia ñ terminatur ·nec includitur nec
excluditur ·Iacet in domo paraliticus
et male torquetur ·Quid ergo uis ·uel
cupis ·seu desideras ·Non multum loquor ait ·scio enī quod ad omiā cogno-
scentē loquor ·ñ uerbosor ·Scio enim
quod ad omiā prescientē respondeo ·
ideoqȝ iste agnoscens corda respondēs
dicit ·ego ueniā et curabo eū ·ego ad
abraham ueniens senilē sare sanaui
uterū in senectute eius ·ysaac filiū do-
nans ·Ego ueniens et nunc ad te curabo eū ·Et quomodo p mittis dr̄ne ad
uentū tuū huic nec queri ·nec peti ·
sciens quod ñ acceptabile sit ei ·ut ueniens in domū eius ·ob hoc ut uos pre
ualeatis et eius fidei similis uel cogno-
scatis quis iste sit ·uel qualis in eo fidei
thesaurus habeatur occultus ·Iam enī
et primitus abraham tēptaui ·non pro
hoc ut cognoscerē quē ipse sciebam ·
sed ut uos ei similes in omi tēptatione ·

arum non occur

perbię · et manuſ

nungat michi · S

rbum tuum · et p

London, British Library, Harley Ms. 7183 (Homilies of Augustine). Written in northern Italy, during the first half of the 12th century.

The page size is 21¾" x 14½" (553 x 370 mm). The manuscript is in two volumes: Volume 1 contains folios 1–154, and Volume 2, folios 155–317. The whole-page reproduction is taken from folio 119v, and the enlargement (three and a half times actual size) from folio 78v, the bottom of the left hand column.

The Caroline minuscule from 9th-century France was copied by scribes all over Europe. But early in the 11th century, signs of Gothic compression and angularity began to appear. In Italy and Spain, however, the rounded Caroline script prevailed. In the 12th century, Italian scribes wrote this bold, but very legible, version of the 9th-century French original. Renaissance scholars, in the 15th century, developed a 'new' style of script, which we now call Humanist minuscule. They turned for their inspiration to the *litera antiqua,* the Caroline minuscules in Italian 12th-century manuscripts like the one illustrated here (see also Introduction, *Fig. 6).*

Harley Ms. 7183 is an impressive manuscript of large proportions. It has very generous margins, and the page is laid out with two columns of text, each column carrying 50 lines. Its script has been much admired. Edward Johnston, in his notes on his plate X *(Writing & Illuminating, & Lettering)* is, uncharacteristically, lavish in his praise: 'This has all the qualities of good writing in a marked degree, and I consider it, taken all around, the most perfect and satisfactory penmanship which I have seen'.

It is certainly a magnificent script, combining soundness of structure with unique character, while preserving the spirit and freedom of writing. Here is an exemplary simplicity of form, and directness of execution. The letters are evenly spaced and the words are clearly separated, but it maintains a strong sense of the line of writing. This is helped by the short ascenders and the wide interlinear space. The hand is largely free from mannerisms, and is very legible.

The manuscript incorporated large, decorative initials, followed by a few lines of Uncials, to mark the beginning of each section. Edward Johnston, with his more usual candour, considers them to be 'comparatively poor, at least, to fall short of the perfection of the manuscript'!

Note the 'Uncial' form of **h**; the frequent use of round **s** at the ends of words; the long **s** which stops at the baseline to distinguish it from **f**; and the upright form of **t**. Note also that the pen angle is generally steeper than that used for the English Caroline minuscules (see *C6).*

a uiui · qui precepto patriſ m

59

xpiannitatiſ & xpianę fidei
ut felix inope locuples in
fide cum rege regum gťe
riſ cui eſt honor & gła p
eterna ſcła ſctorum a oħ

Cum datur ſceptrum

Accipe ſceptrum regię
poteſtatiſ inſigne uir
gam ſcilicet regni rectam
uirgam uirtutiſ qua te ip
ſum bene regaſ ſcam ecclia
poptinq; uidelicet xpianū
tibi a deo comiſſum regia
uirtute ab impbiſ defendaſ

ccipe regie dignitatisa
lum · & phunc in te cai
fidei signaculū · quia u
hie ordinari · caput & p
regni ac populi · ita pfe

London, British Library, Cotton Ms. Tiberius B. viii (Office Book of Episcopal Rites). Written in southern England, most probably by Eadwine, scribe of Christ Church, Canterbury, *c.* 1150–1160.

The page size size is 11⅜" x 7½" (290 x 191 mm). The manuscript has 196 folios. This manuscript bears the same Cotton shelf mark as the illustrated account of the Coronation of Charles V, which was written in France in 1365. These two quite distinct volumes are now bound separately, volume I consists of folios 1–34 plus 81–196 and volume 2, folios 35–80. The whole-page reproduction is taken from folio 95v, and the enlargement (twice actual size) from 95R.

Teresa Webber identifies the scribe of this manuscript as the principal scribe of the Eadwine Psalter (Cambridge, Trinity College, Ms. R. 17. 1). That Psalter was written at Christ Church, Canterbury during the 1150's, and the principal scribe was most probably Eadwine himself – the self-styled 'Prince of Scribes'. Canterbury was an important centre for manuscript production during the 11th and 12th centuries. That vigorous and sustained output resulted in a recognizable, mid 12th-century, Christ Church 'house style', seen in

the script illustrated here. This hand has much in common with that of an earlier scribe, also from Christ Church, Eadui Basan (see *C8*). Both scripts have an upright, rounded aspect, and similar forms of **&** and **a** (note the long, hairline entrance stroke). Pen rotation is also evident in both hands.

The transition from Caroline minuscules to Gothic scripts did not happen overnight. The characteristics of Gothic bookhands are lateral compression, heavy weight and sharp angularity. The beginnings of compression can be seen in the script of Eadui, but in the 12th-century hand seen here there are also strong hints of Gothic angularity, in addition to the clearly evident compression and heavy weight. (Different styles of Protogothic can be seen in *D2* and *E5*.)

Note the varied pen angle, generally slanted; the detailed serifs on the ascenders; the waistline serifs of **i, m, n, p, r** and **u**; and the foot serifs sometimes made with an added stroke. The sections are marked by pen-made Versal capitals, written in red.

uerabif auctor ac ftat

61

De curia de Lathem.

Ego Balduinus flandrie ⁊ hañoe comes. ⁊ kᵃrma
conuinx mea. varia comitissa. cognitum ēē
uolumus tam p̄sentibȝ qᵐ futuris. noɓ ue
raciter innotuisse. eiudeū di g̃a abbem monasterij
bi Bauonis. de consensu totus capli curiã suam
Lathem dc̄am. cum appendicijs suis ⁊ tribȝ p̄bendis.
d̄ne margarete custracen̄ castellane. pie in x̄po fa
miliaritatis intuitu. ad usum uite sue simplicit̃
commodasse. retenta in omnibȝ ad opus sū Bauonis
apptietate. Pred̄am siquidem margareta. p̄ceptis ecclie
beneficijs condigne uolens respondere. q̄cq̄o tam
in edificijs. qᵐ in possessionibȝ. siue nutritus ani
malium. uel quolibȝ m̄ ex eius conq̄sitoē ⁊ aug
m̄taroē eide curie usum fuerit accreuisse. ad sa
lutem anime sue p̄merendam. monasrio bi Bauo
nis iusto donatois tᵼtulo rtulit in elemosinam
perpetuo possidēdam. Vñde nulli mortaliū ulla
c̄sanguinitatis uel affinitatis p̄pinq̄tate. uel alia
qualibet occasione. tam in bonis iam d̄c̄e margᵼ.
quoad uixerit tantum c̄ōmodatis. qᵐ in rebȝ ex
ctie in elemosinā libere collatis. q̄c̄qᵐ iuris ute
rius require licitum erit. Ad hanc ᵹ donaroē.
qᵐ ego ⁊ kᵃrma ouinx mea. os. comitissa sollemp
niter frām ecclie p̄sentes agnouimus modis oībȝ

The St Bavo Cartulary. London, British Library, Add. Ms. 16952 (Monastic records). Written late in the 12th century at the Abbey of St Bavo in Ghent.

The page size is 10⅝" x 7⅜" (271 x 188 mm). The manuscript has 52 folios. The whole-page reproduction and the enlargement (four times actual size) are taken from folio 14R, showing the Charter of Ego Baldvinus.

Originally compiled and written late in the 12th century, the manuscript contains Charters and Deeds relating to the Abbey from the year AD 819 onwards. Entries in various later hands have been added, on folios 37–52, up to the year 1344. It is written in pale brown gall ink and has Versal initials decorated with line work in contrasting colours, red and green.

The hand of the Cartulary reveals a transitional stage between the earlier, rounded Caroline minuscule and the fully developed, angular Gothic scripts. In addition to the lateral compression and heavy weight of the letters, there are also (as in the 'Eadwine' Protogothic script, *D1*) hints of angularity, especially in the arched forms. Other Gothic traits can be seen in this manuscript. The ascenders are short and the foot serifs of **m** and **n** are rather flat – a

feature anticipating the character of later Prescissus hands. There are also instances here (not seen in *D1*) of the 'biting of bows' (see *D3* notes). Note **bb** (line 4 opposite), **pp** (line 6) and, more unusually, **ar** (line 7). Note also the decorative capitals used in the title, **D** and **L**. Others in the text, **B** (line 5) and **P** (line 10), have pointed tops similar to later Gothic capitals. Some lowercase letters have alternative forms, (eg. **d**, **m**, **r**, **s** and **v**). The character which looks like a figure 7 is a Gothic form of ampersand.

For an illustration of folio 12R of this manuscript see the catalogue *The Universal Penman,* page 9. Some of the larger initials on that page, very heavy, double-stroke Versals, have been left open and unfilled. Ewan Clayton detects the origins of open Gothic capitals in such letters. Also on that page is a rare instance, in 12th-century texts, of the letter **w**. Perhaps the earliest occurrence of **w** is seen in a late 11th-century manuscript (see *Western Historical Scripts* by Michelle Brown, plate 24 and notes thereon).

63

prouidentiam. et animarum pro
curationem? ut per diuine legis i
cedendo precepta. sis ei dux ad celes
tis hereditatis pascua. adiuuante
domino nostro ihu xpo. Qui cu
patre. Tunc det ei eps uirgam pas
toralem dicens.

ccipe uirgam pastoralem sol
licitudinis. et sic uigila su
per gregem dominicum tibi comis
sum. quatinus sicut fidelis seruus
et prudens. merearis intrare in gau
dium domini tui. Si autem pbr
ordinatus est altas. det ei eps bal

The Metz Pontifical. Cambridge, Fitzwilliam Museum, Ms. 298. Written and illuminated in northeastern France for Raymond de Bar, who was Bishop of Metz from 1306–1316.

The page size is 12½" x 9¾" (317 x 250mm, somewhat trimmed from the original format). The manuscript has 140 folios. The whole-page reproduction is taken from folio 81R and the enlargement (one and a half times actual size) is from folio 90v. Another part of this Pontifical is in Prague University Library, Ms. XXIII. C. 120.

This lavish manuscript was probably produced in the same workshop as the Verdun Breviary (London, British Library, Yates Thompson Ms. 8, volume 1; volume 2 is in Verdun). It was undoubtedly intended for ceremonial rather than actual liturgical use. Many of the pages devote half their space to highly finished miniatures, with much use of raised and burnished gold of extraordinary quality and brightness. As in other Gothic manuscripts, the heavy weight of the writing is matched by the appearance of the paintings. From folio 98R on, some decorations are unfinished, with preparatory drawings rendered in pale ink, providing valuable insights into the methods of the medieval illuminator.

The hallmarks of Gothic scripts are lateral compression, heavy weight and angular forms. From *c.* 1180 onwards, fully developed Gothic bookhands also began the 'biting of bows'. This describes the linking of certain letter pairs by a shared stem. It most commonly occurs when **b**, 'Uncial' **d**

or **p** are followed by the vowels **a**, **e** or **o**. This manuscript, however, also includes pairs beginning with **h**, eg. **he** (line 4), **ho** and even **ha**. Note the 'triplet' of letters **bba** (line 14). In many Gothic scripts the ascenders and descenders tend to be short, and this allows the lines of text to be closer together. In the Metz Pontifical, the x-height equals the interlinear space, excluding ascenders and descenders.

This large and very expert Quadrata script is written with great sensitivity and rhythm especially by the scribe whose hand is seen from folio 63R onwards. It retains a hint of the earlier roundness in some of its forms. This 'softens' its appearance, and helps it to avoid the lifelessness and mechanical rigidity of many 'blackletter' hands. It is written very sharply; few medieval manuscripts have such crisp forms and fine hairlines as this one.

Note the differing slopes of the diagonal strokes; the unusual built-up wedge serifs of the **i** and **u**; the use of both long and short **s**; and the change of pen angle needed to complete the terminations of ascenders and descenders. The illustrations include a number of examples of Gothic capitals: **N**, **Q**, **S** and **T**.

Benedicite angeli domini dño: benedicite celi domino

Benedicite aque omnes que super celos sunt dño: benedicite omnes virtutes domini domino

Benedicite sol z luna domino: benedicite stelle celi domino

Benedicite ymber z ros domino: benedicite omnes spc dei dño

Benedicite ignis z estus domino: benedicite frigus z estas domino

Benedicite rores z pruina domino: benedicite gelu z frigus dño.

Benedicite glacies z niues dño: benedicite noctes z dies dño

Benedicite lux z tenebre dño: benedi

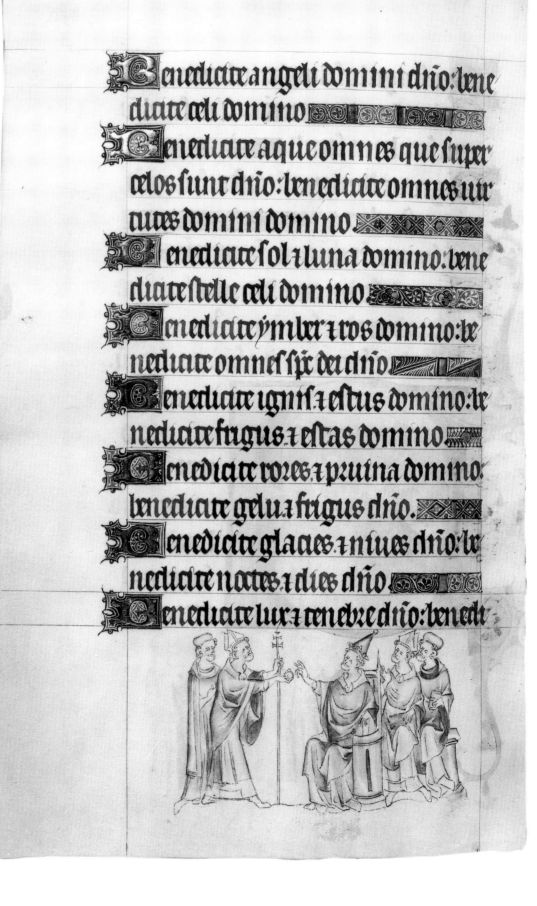

The Queen Mary Psalter. London, British Library, Royal Ms. 2. B. vii (Latin Psalter with canticles). Written in England, sometime between 1310 and 1320, and illuminated by a single (anonymous) artist who may have been in charge of a workshop in London. In the 16th century the manuscript was impounded by a customs officer and presented by him to Mary Tudor.

The page size is 11" x 6⅞" (280 x 175 mm). The manuscript has 460 folios. The whole-page reproduction and the enlargement (two and a half times actual size) are both taken from folio 294v, which shows part of the Benedicite.

This Psalter has line and wash drawings at the foot of each page, and many richly decorated miniature paintings, with much use of raised and burnished gold. This variation of Gothic script is called 'prescissus' because of its use of abrupt baseline terminations to certain letters, eg. most instances of **f**, **m**, **n** and long **s**. The extra effort required for this formal finishing made this script suitable for only the most luxurious of manuscripts. The script of this Psalter would need considerable manipulation of the pen to make the lower, 'dished' terminals. Most other prescissus scripts have square-cut endings (see *E6*). Despite this inconvenience, this script maintains a commendable liveliness and rhythm. Other examples of this style, such as the Luttrell Psalter (British Library, Add. Ms. 42130), tend to be over-precise and therefore rather mechanical.

Note the alternative forms for **d**, **i**, **m**, **n**, **r** and **s**; the whimsical dotting of the **i**; the typical Gothic 'biting of bows'; and the **&** (it looks rather like a figure 7). Note also the extremely heavy Versal initials and line endings which are matched by the weight of the text writing.

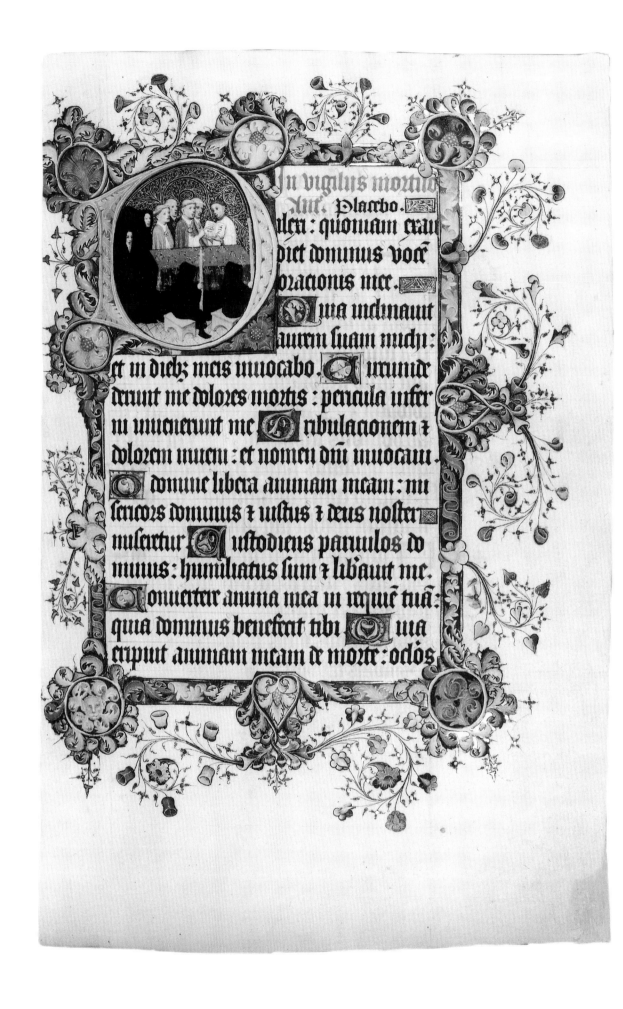

In vigilijs mortuo
Ant. Placebo.
alri : quoniam exau
diet dominus voce
oracionis mee.
Quia inclinauit
aurem suam michi :
et in diebz meis inuocabo. Cirumde
derunt me dolores mortis : pericula infer
ni inuenerunt me. Tribulacionem z
dolorem inueni : et nomen dni inuocaui.
O domine libera animam meam : mi
sericors dominus z iustus z deus noster
miseretur. Custodiens paruulos do
minus : humiliatus sum z libauit me.
Conuertere anima mea in requiem tuã :
quia dominus benefecit tibi. Quia
eripuit animam meam de morte : oclos

The Bedford Hours and Psalter. London, British Library, Add. Ms. 42131 (Liturgical service book). Written and lavishly illuminated before 1423 for John, Duke of Bedford (1389–1435), in the London workshop of Herman Scheere. The manuscript is signed on folio 124R, 'Herman your meeke servant'.

The page size 16⅛" x 10¾" (410 x 273 mm). The manuscript has 40 folios. The whole-page reproduction and the enlargement (twice actual size) are both taken from folio 46R.

The decline of legibility in later Gothic scripts, is well illustrated by this example. The characteristic lateral compression, heavy weight, and sharp angularity are here pushed to their limits, giving the appearance of interlacing – hence the name 'textura'. Many of the letters appear to be constructed with a number of almost identical vertical strokes, uniformly spaced. This rigidity, together with the rather conspicuous lozenge-shaped terminations enhance the decorative aspect of the writing, but make it very difficult to read to our modern eyes, and no doubt the eyes of Italian Humanists.

Nevertheless, the script used in the Bedford Hours and Psalter is expertly executed. It is written very slowly and precisely, with many pen lifts. The lozenge-shaped terminations are made with a separate stroke overlapping the upright, and at the baseline are often elongated to a point. The 'forked' ascenders require the use of the corner of the pen. Note the steep pen angle; and the alternative forms of **a**, **d**, **r** and **s**. The Gothic 'biting of bows' (see *D3* notes) are here limited to **de** and **do**. The weighty appearance of the historiated initial and the Versal capitals is again matched by the heavy script (see *D4*).

est daller aux peuples des citez et bonnes villes ain
si que ie voy que la plusgrant partie se gouuerne
presentement me veul oultrement excuser pour
les rudesses orgueil rebellion et estranges manieres
quilz tiennent en beaucop de lieux Et les aucuns
a locasion des guerres et oultrages que lon leur
fait sont si pacionnez traueilles et greuez quilz
ont perdu come toute congnoissance de raison.
Or regardez tresnoble dame se les raisons q̃
ie vous ay par remonstrees me font bien a penser
Mais se vous seulement me comandes de aller p
deuers tant particulieres come a gens deglise
princes nobles ou personnages des comunautez
des citez et bonnes villes En ce cas ie ne me rende
roie point difficile car il en est et ie en congnois
de si sardes prudens et bien aprins en bonte et hu
milite desquelz ie me oseroie bien fier deulx dire
et remonstrer toutes choses comuenables et honno
rables esquelz a tant de perfection que ce q̃ ie le²
diroie Ilz le treuueroient en bien come ie croy Et
toutesfois finablemet tresnoble dame quelq̃ pro
testacion ou excusacion que iay par cy deuãt faicte
puis que vous le me conseilliez quoy quil men
doie aduenir a laide de m̃seigneur Ie suy prest
dacomplir vostre requeste que ie veul retenir

London, British Library, Royal Ms. 19. C. viii *(Imaginacion de Vraye Noblesse).* Written probably in Ghent or Bruges, *c.* 1496. (This manuscript was presented in 1496 to Henry VII of England by Quintin Poulet, his librarian.)

The page size is 12¼" x 8½" (310 x 215 mm). The manuscript has 97 folios. The whole-page reproduction is taken from folio 7R and the enlargement (three times actual size) from folio 43V.

Alongside the formal Gothic hands, there existed in the 14th and 15th centuries numerous cursive scripts used for legal, commercial and other documents. Bâtarde is a bookhand which evolved, initially in northern France, as a formalized version of one of these Gothic cursives. Variations of the script appeared in England and elsewhere, and its popularity can be judged by the fact that it provided the basis for a number of early typefaces in France and England (eg. for William Caxton's 1483 edition of *The Canterbury Tales).*

In Flanders, at the end of the 15th century, Bâtarde was used, often at large scale, for luxury volumes written in French to meet the growing demands of wealthy and aristocratic bibliophiles. This manuscript is a typical example, lavishly illuminated and richly bound.

The script also appears stylish and confident – almost arrogant. It is written fairly slowly and is full of mannerisms and self-conscious vanities. Note the great flourish given to f and long s, and the tapering (nearly non-existent) descenders, especially on y (line 2, letter 10, opposite).

Gothic Bâtarde is written with a very flexible pen (the heavy f and long s are apparently the result of pen pressure) and the strong textural quality is enhanced by its forward slope. The pen angle, about 30°, is flatter than that used for more formal Gothics. For the pointed curves, however, it is nearer to 40°. Some other letters need an even steeper pen angle or the use of the corner of the pen.

There are some variant forms, including two styles of **r**, long and short **s**, and round and pointed **v** (the latter used only at the beginnings of words). Legibility is hindered by the numerous idiosyncratic forms. For example, the middle word in line 1 (above) is not 'tax' but 'car'; and the word toward the end of line 5 (above) is not 'foeʙ' but 'Roeʙ'. The **q** (line 2, letter 3, opposite) could be mistaken for a **g**, and the **x** (line 1, letter 12) for a flourished **v**. The **z** form (end of line 7) is used interchangeably, at word endings, for either **s**, **x** or **z**.

The elaborate initials used within the text are, in fact, illuminated 'pilcrows'. This decorative form of the Greek letter pi (Π) was traditionally used, in both manuscripts and printed books, to signify the beginning of paragraphs.

INCIPIT
PRAEFA-
TIO SCI
HIERONI
MI PRAES
BYTERI
IN VETE
RI TESTA
MENTO.

ES[I]
DE
RII
MEI
DE
SI
DE
RA
TAS
ACCE
PI EPIS
TO LAS.
QUI QUOD A
PRAESAGIO
FUTURORUM.

CUM DANIHELE SORTITUS EST NOMEN
OBSECRANTIS. UT TRANSLATUM
IN LATINAM LINGUAM DE HEBREO
SERMONE PENTATEUCHUM NOSTRO
RUM AURIBUS TRADEREM
PERICULOSUM OPUS CERTE OBTREC
TATORUM LATRATIBUS PATENS
QUI ME ASSERUNT IN SEPTUAGIN
TA INTERPRAETUM SUCCILLATIO
NEM NOUA PRO UETERIBUS CUDE
RE. ITA INGENIUM QUASI UINUM PRO
BANTES. CUM EGO SAEPISSIME TES
TATUS SIM ME PRO UILI PORTIONE
IN TABERNACULO DI OFFERRE QUAE
POSSIM. NEC OPES ALTERIUS ALIORU
PAUPERTATE FEDARI. QUOD UT AUDE
REM ORIGENIS ME STUDIUM PROUO
CAUIT. QUI EDITIONI ANTIQUAE TRANS
LATIONE THEODOTIONIS MISCUIT
ASTERISCO. ET OBELO. ID E STELLA ET UERU
OPUS OMNE DISTINGUENS. DUM AUT IN LU
CESCERE FACIT QUAE MINUS ANTE FUERANT
AUT SUPERFLUA QUAEQ IUGULAT ET CON
FODIT. MAXIME QUAE EUANGELISTARU
ET APOSTOLORUM AUCTORITAS PRO
MULGAUIT. IN QUIBUS MULTA DE UETE
RI TESTAMENTO LEGIMUS QUAE IN NOS
TRIS CODICIBUS NON HABENTUR UT E
ILLUD EX AECYPTO UOCAUI FILIUM MEU
ET QNM NAZAREUS UOCABITUR ET UI
DEBUNT IN QUEM CONPUNXERUNT
ET FLUMINA DE UENTRE EIUS FLUENT
AQUAE UIUAE ET QUAE NEC OCULUS UIDIT
NEC AURIS AUDIUIT. NEC IN COR HOMI
NIS ASCENDIT. QUAE PRAEPARAUIT

PRAEFA

TIO SC

HIERON

BYTERI

Munich, Bayerische Staatsbibliothek, CLM. 12741 (Latin Vulgate Bible in one volume). Written at the Abbey of St Martin, Tours, France, *c.* AD 830.

The page size is 20¼" x 14⅞" (512 x 378 mm). The manuscript has 253 folios – about 40 are missing at the end. The whole-page reproduction and the enlargement (one and a half times actual size) are both taken from folio 4R, which shows part of Jerome's Preface to the Old Testament.

This magnificent manuscript is one of nearly 100 Bibles produced at St Martin's between the years 800 and 850 (see *C5* notes).

Built-up, compound capitals, based on Roman monumental lettering had already been used in earlier manuscripts (see Introduction, *Fig. 8* and *Fig. 9)*, but it was Carolingian scribes who perfected their use. Certainly, the influence of classical inscriptions can be seen clearly in the elegant proportions and very open spacing of the written

capitals in this manuscript. They rival even those in the Metz Gospels (Paris, Bibliothèque Nationale, Ms. Lat. 9388), and are more expert than those in the other well-known Bibles from St Martin's, the Moutier Grandval *(C5)* and the Vivian (Paris, Bibliothèque Nationale, Ms. Lat. 1). However, the large, interlaced initial, in the Franco-Saxon style, perhaps overpowers the balance of this otherwise graceful, if austere, page.

The capital letters were undoubtedly written in outline with a narrow pen, and then the body of the main stems filled in. Note the backward tilt given to the inner ellipse of the rounded letters and the slight entasis of the main stems – both features reminiscent of classical Roman inscriptions. The serifs, however, have been adapted to a more calligraphic form. Some of the capitals (eg. **M**, **N**, **V** and perhaps **A**) are rather too wide for true classical proportions. The Greek **Y** form is certainly too slight. The show-through from folio 4v reveals the capital height and writing line relationship.

The Second Bible of Charles the Bald. Paris, Bibliothèque
Nationale, Ms. Lat. 2 (Latin Vulgate Bible in one volume).
Written at the Abbey of St Amand, northeast of Paris,
between AD 871 and 877.

    The page size is 17" x 13¼" (430 x 335 mm). The manu-
script has 444 folios. The whole-page reproduction is taken
from folio 10V, which shows the Incipit for the Book of
Genesis, and the detail (actual size) from folio 354V, part
of the Matthew Incipit.

Unlike the Bibles from the Abbey of St Martin, Tours – the
(First) Bible of Charles the Bald, sometimes known as the
Vivian Bible (Paris, Bibliothèque Nationale, Ms. Lat. 1) and
the Moutier Grandval Bible *(C5)* – this Bible has little
figurative decoration. A product of the so-called Franco-
Saxon School, it relies on a classical simplicity – beautiful
'monumental' capitals with a restrained use of interlacing.

Each book within the Bible has a decorative opening. The
First Book of Samuel, the Psalms and the Epistle to the
Romans begin with a whole page of capitals. The Old
Testament (Genesis) and the New Testament (Matthew)
open with a double-page spread of large capitals, the title on
the left and the first words of the book on the right. (The
recto page facing the one reproduced opposite appears as
plate 48 of *Carolingian Painting.)* On both pages of the
Matthew opening (folios 354V and 355R), the capitals stand
alone, without decorative borders.

    These elegant capitals were gilded and then outlined in
vermilion. They owe their fundamental character, proportion and spacing to classical Roman inscriptions, probably
seen at first hand by the scribe. The weight and serif formation, however, have been adapted to calligraphic form and
the design requirements – capitals on other, less important,
pages are smaller and comparatively heavier.

DS
QVIHODI
ERNADIE
DISCIPV
LORUM

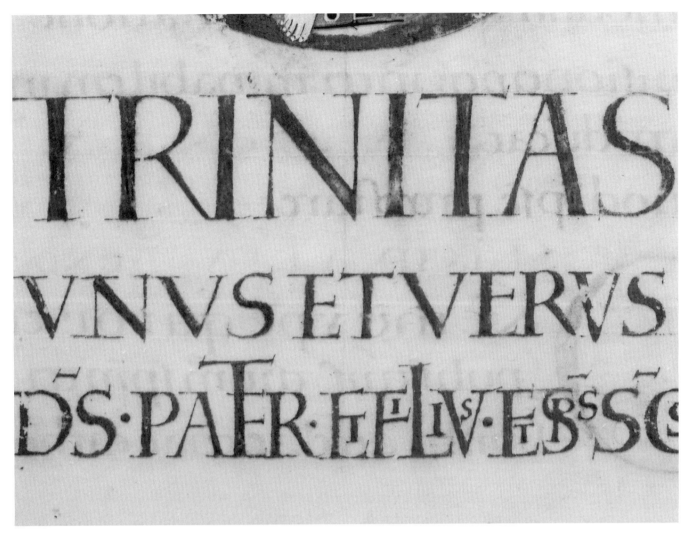

The Benedictional of Aethelwold. London, British Library, Add. Ms. 49598 (Episcopal liturgical blessings). Written in Winchester, AD 971–984 (see the notes on *C7*).

The page size is 11½" x 8½" (292 x 216 mm). The manuscript has 119 folios. The whole-page reproduction is taken from folio 68R, and the enlargement (one and a half times actual size) from folio 70R.

A poem written at the beginning of the manuscript records that Godeman was instructed by Aethelwold, Bishop of Winchester, to write and illuminate this Benedictional for the Bishop's own use. It was to have 'many frames well-adorned and filled with various figures decorated with numerous beautiful colours and with gold'.

Many such pages adorn this manuscript. Usually the decorative frames, like the one shown opposite, contain the opening words of the various solemn Episcopal Blessings. Those words are drawn with a pen in the distinctive English version of the earlier Caroline capitals. They take their inspiration from the use of the pen rather than from classical inscriptional letters, being vigorously and directly written – especially the smaller capitals – with a minimum of preliminary planning. Unlike the capitals of *E1*, they have simplified, naturally written serifs.

Edward Johnston called these capitals, and all the built-up, compound-stroke capitals derived from them, Versals. (This term was apparently first used by E F Strange in his book *Alphabets*, to denote the type of manuscript capitals used to mark the beginning of *verses* and paragraphs.)

Versals are 'built-up' capitals; they are made with many pen strokes. For most of the broad stems the outer strokes would be drawn first, and then the space between them filled. Narrow stems would be made with single strokes of the pen; the vertical stem of **N** suggests the size of the pen used for these letters. For horizontal crossbars on **E, F, H, L** and **T** the pen would be turned sideways, to almost a 90° pen angle. The capitals are in gold throughout the manuscript. First, using size, the letters were outlined with a pen, and the wider strokes filled in. Finally, the letters were overlaid with gold.

The enlargement from folio 70R exhibits a show-through of text from folio 70V. This shows how the size of the capitals, and their interlinear space, related to the line of writing. Note that the letters are not governed by Roman inscriptional proportions (cf. the width of **A** and **S** above with those in *A2).* They vary according to their size, the available space (see the different widths of **V** above) and the judgement of the scribe.

INCIPIT
EVANGELIVM
SECVNDVM
MARCVM:

EXPLICIT BREVIARIVS ·

INCIPIT :

EVANGELIVM :

SECVNDVM :

IOHANNEM ⸓

The Trinity Gospels. Cambridge, Trinity College Library, Ms. B. 10. 4 (the Four Gospels in Latin). Written in southern England, possibly at Christ Church, Canterbury in the first quarter of the 11th century.

The page size is 12⅞" x 9¼" (328 x 235 mm). The manuscript has 174 folios. The whole-page reproduction is taken from folio 59R (showing the Incipit for Mark's Gospel), and the detail (actual size) is taken from folio 132R (the Incipit for John's Gospel).

This is one of the most magnificent Gospel Books to have survived from the 10th or 11th centuries. It is richly illuminated with gold and colour. An elaborate, full-page portrait of Christ in Majesty precedes the Gospels (see the colour illustration in *The Golden Age of Anglo-Saxon Art,* plate 13). Each of the four title pages, in brightly gilded Versal capitals, are followed by individual portraits of the Evangelists. These are surrounded by ornamented frames, in a style reminiscent of Winchester manuscripts (compare *E3*). Large decorative initials, and gold capitals are seen at the beginning of each Gospel.

The main scribe of this manuscript may have been a contemporary of Eadui Basan at Christ Church (see *C8).* Like Eadui, he is known to have contributed to a number of other manuscripts. This scribe wrote all of the Jumièges Missal (Rouen, Bibliothèque Municipale, Ms. Y. 6), most of

British Library, Royal Ms. 1. D. ix, and he also finished the Copenhagen Gospels (Copenhagen, Kongelige Bibliotek, Ms. Gl. Kgl. Sml. 10, 2°) which had been started in the 10th century. Links with these other books suggest a connection with Christ Church (there are Eadui notes in the Royal manuscript), and also with Peterborough Abbey, founded by Aethelwold. (The Jumièges Missal copied texts first used at Peterborough.)

The Versal capitals in the Trinity Gospels are of outstanding quality. Despite their variable proportions and slightly uneven weight, they are confidently made and full of character. Brightly gilded and surrounded by generous margins, these capitals create an impressive page. They are slightly heavier that the Aethelwold Versals *(E3),* matching the heavier text script of the Gospels, and perhaps, also indicating a move towards the Early Gothic style.

Note that in order to make these compound capitals, many strokes of a narrow pen are used and its angle must be continually modified according to the stroke being made. Note the flat-topped **A, M,** and **N**; the very wide **C** and **G**; the superb **O**; the heavy crossbar on **A** and especially **H**. The backward lean of **C, G,** and **S** could perhaps be adjusted. Note also the whimsical arrangement of letters on folio 59R, which is done in order to achieve a 'fit'.

79

EXPLICIVNT.
CAPITVLA.
INCIPIT.
MALACHIM.
I. LIBER.
REGVM.

.TERCIVS.

habebatq; erat plurimos dies. Cumq; opi reretur uestibus. non calefiebat. Dixerunt g serui sui. Queramus dno nro regi adolescen tulam uirginem. & stet coram rege & foueat eum. dormiatq; in sinu suo. & calefaciat dnm nrm regem. Quesierunt igitur adolescentulam speciosam in omnibz finibus isrl. & inuenerunt abisag sunamiten. & adduxerunt eam ad regem. Erat aute puella pulchra nimis. dormiebatq; cum rege. & ministrabat ei. Rex uero non cogno uit eam. Adonias aute filius agith. eleuabat dicens. Ego regnabo. Fecitq; sibi currus & equi tes. & quinquaginta uiros qui ante eum curre rent. nec corripuit eum pater suus aliquando dicens. Quare hoc fecisti. Erat autem & ipse pulcher ualde. secundus natu post absalon. Er sermo fuit cu ioab filio saruie. & cu abiathar sacerdote. qui adiuuabant partes adonie. Sadoc uero sacerdos. & banaias filius ioiade. & nathan ppheta. & cerethi & felethi. & robur exercitus dauid. non erat cum adonia. Immola uit ergo adonias arietibus & uitulis. & uniuersis pinguibus iuxta lapidem zoeleth. qui erat in cinus fontis rogel. uocauit uniuersos fres suos filios regis. & omnes uiros iuda seruos regis. Nathan autem pphetam & banaiam & robustos quosq; & salomone frem suum non uocauit. Dixit itaq; nathan ad bethsabee matre salomonis. Num audisti quod regnauerit adonias filius agith. & dns nr dauid hoc ignorat. Nunc ergo ueni & accipe a me consilium. & salua anima tua filiiq; tui salomonis. Vade & ingredere ad regem dauid. & dic ei. Nonne tu dne mi rex iurasti mihi ancille tue dicens. quod salomon filius tuus regnabit post me. & ipse sedebit in solio meo. Quare ergo regnat adonias. Et adhuc

The Winchester Bible. Winchester, Cathedral Library (Latin Vulgate Bible in four volumes). Written soon after 1160 at St Swithun's Priory, Winchester. Bishop Henry de Blois (1129–1171) encouraged the production of books – this Bible must have been the Cathedral's greatest undertaking.

The page size is 22¾" x 15¾" (578 x 400 mm). The manuscript has 468 folios. Originally in two volumes, it is now bound in four. The whole-page reproduction and the enlargement (one and a half times actual size) are both taken from folio 109R, which shows the beginning of the First Book of Kings.

This is but one of several lavish Bibles produced in the 12th century. Others include the Bury Bible (Cambridge, Corpus Christi College Library, Ms. 2) and the Lambeth Bible (Lambeth Palace Library, Ms. 3). These and the Winchester Bible are renowned for their magnificent miniature paintings, which make extravagant use of gold and a full range of colours, including the very rare and precious lapis lazuli. Six or seven professional artists, some perhaps from Sicily and Spain, were commissioned to illuminate the Winchester Bible. As it was never completed, the unfinished pages give a fascinating insight into the methods of the medieval scribe and illuminator.

In these Bibles Versal letters were used for the opening words of the individual books. As they were often fitted around the imposing historiated initials, they sometimes suffered distortion and contraction. On folio 109R, however, the scribe has had adequate room for the long colophon. This allows us to see undistorted letterforms with generous letter spacing.

The weight of these robust, compound capitals (written in alternate lines of red and blue) matches the heaviness of the illumination and the Protogothic script of the text (cf. *D1*) written almost entirely by one scribe. The capitals are occasionally relieved by decorative detail. Note that the bowl of the **B** and similar letters is not formed horizontally from the vertical stem, as in the Benedictional *(E3)*, but curves upward and downward from it. Later 'Lombardic' Versals (see *E6*) exaggerate this tendency even further. Note also the size of the letters in relation to the text lines; the imaginative variations of **A**; and the 'Uncial' variants of **E**, **H** and **M**. The **N**, compared to the weight of the other letters, is rather weak.

stituisti me.

5 ✠ **V**erba mea auribz pcipe dñe:
intellige clamorem meum.
Intende uoci orationis mee: rex m̃s
et deus meus.
Qm̃ ad te orabo dñe: mane exaudi
es uocem meam.
Mane astabo t̃ et uidebo: qm̃ non ds
uolens iniquitatem tu es.
Neqz habitabit iuxta te malign̄: neqz
pmanebunt iniusti ante oculos
tuos.
Odisti omnes qui opant̄ iniquitate:
pdes omnes qui loquunt̄ m̃edaciū.
Virum sanguinum et dolosum ab
hominabitur dñs: ego autem in
m̃ltitudine mĩe tue.
Introibo in domum tuam: adora
bo ad templ̃m s̃c̃m tuum in timo
re tuo.

a

b

c

d

e

The Amesbury Psalter. Oxford, All Souls College Library, Ms. 6 (Latin Psalter of Sarum Use). Written in Salisbury, southern England, *c.* 1250, probably for the Convent of Amesbury.

The page size is 12" x 8½" (305 x 215 mm). The manuscript has 186 folios. The whole-page reproduction is from folio 15v and the enlargements (one and a half times actual size) are from folio 14v (**a**, **b** and **d**), folio 143R (**c**), and folio 149v (**e**).

The illuminations are attributed to one main artist, the 'Sarum (ie. Salisbury) Master', and his followers. At least three other manuscripts are known to have been produced by this artist, including the Wilton Psalter (now at the Royal College of Physicians).

As the Gothic period progressed, text scripts became more angular and much heavier. The boldness of the text was matched by the stronger weight of the display capitals; producing in extreme examples, rather obese and often

crudely-distorted letters. Edward Johnston, and others, refer to these bold and ornate form of Versals as 'Lombardic', though an actual connection to Lombardy in Italy seems highly unlikely.

In the Amesbury Psalter, however, the Versal capitals are vigorous and strong. Their boldness of weight is relieved by the delicacy and inventiveness of the filigree line-work. The letters are rendered alternately in red and blue, and the line work is drawn in the opposite, contrasting colour.

Here, in this manuscript we also encounter the typical use of Versals as marginal, verse-marking initials. The majority of the capitals have a circular basis, guided here by the squares created by the line ruling for text and margins.

Note the exaggerated curves on the letter **B** (see *E5* note). 'Lombardic' letters are far removed from the classical proportions and elegant capitals of 9th-century France (see *E1* and *E2*).

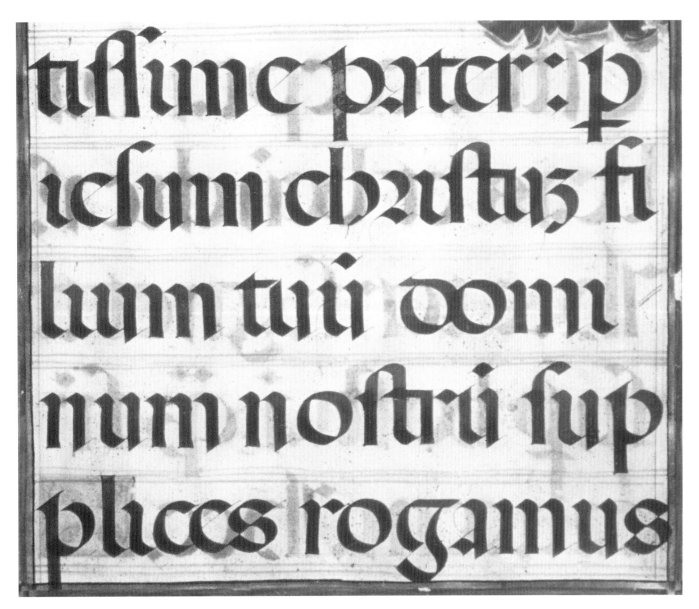

The Carvajal Missal. In a European private collection (Mass book for the Feast of the Epiphany). Written in Rome in *c.*1520 for Bernardino de Carvajal.

The page size is 17⅜" x 12½" (441 x 316 mm). The manuscript has 90 folios. The whole-page reproduction is taken from folio 5R, and the detail (actual size) from folio 46R.

This sumptuous manuscript was made for Cardinal Carvajal, Spanish Ambassador to the court of Rome – his arms occur on folio 5R (opposite). It was probably intended for the Feast of the Epiphany (6th January) in 1521. The extremely elaborate illumination (note the *trompe l'oeil* torn-page effect at the head) is probably by Matteo da Milano, who also contributed illuminations to *F3* and *F5*.

In Spain and Italy, rigidly angular Gothic scripts were largely avoided. In their place evolved 'Rotunda', a hand which was truly Gothic but more rounded in character. It carried the weight and texture of other Gothic hands, but not their excessive compression and sharp angularity. It was widely used, ranging from tiny, personal Books of Hours to

enormous ceremonial liturgical manuscripts (which, like this one, often contained musical notation).

The Carvajal Missal is an outstanding example of a large Gothic Rotunda script, written in black between triple line ruling in pale red. The hand is sharp, precise and strongly structured. A fairly consistent pen angle, about 30°, is used throughout. Close study reveals the use of the corner of the pen to finish the flattened stem endings on **f**, **h**, **m**, **n**, **p**, **r**, and long **s**. Note the rather whimsical back stroke of **g** (which might be improved by straightening); and the two different forms of **d**, **r**, and **s**. The character that looks like a figure 3, line 2 (above), is the contraction for m.

INTERPRETATIO EVSE
BII CAESARIENSIS ED
TA PER BEATVM HIERO
NYMVM; ET IPSIVS PRO
SPERIQ ADDITIONES
DE TEMPORIBVS,

PROLOGVS BEATI HIERONYMI

VSEBIVS
HIERONY
MVS VIN
CENTIO ET
GALIENO
SVIS SALVTEM,
VETVS ISTE DISER
TORVM MOS FVIT VT

CAESARIEN.

PER BEATVM

MVM; ET IPSI

RIQ'ADDITIO

London, British Library, Royal Ms. 14. C. iii (The *Chronicle* of Eusebius in Jerome's Latin version). Written in northern Italy, late in the 15th century, by Bartolomeo San Vito.

The page size is 13" x 9" (330 x 215 mm). The manuscript has 150 folios. The whole-page reproduction and the enlargement (two and a half times actual size) are both taken from folio 2R, which is the title page of the book.

This lavish volume is typical of the many classical texts transcribed for wealthy clients in the latter part of the 15th century. San Vito wrote competent minuscule and Italic hands, but he is best known for his distinctive and elegant Square capitals. He used them in many manuscripts, other than this one, including a Virgil (British Library, Kings Ms. 24), a Petrarch (Victoria & Albert Museum, Ms. L. 101–1947) and a Martial (Bodleian Library, Ms. Auct. F. 4. 33).

It has been noted that from about 1465, Humanist scribes began to give their manuscript capitals a more classical look. At that time in the Renaissance, there was a growing antiquarian interest in ancient inscriptions. The biographer of the Paduan artist, Andrea Mantegna, sketches a romantic vignette of Felice Feliciano, Mantegna, and others as they wandered along the shores of Lake Garda in the Autumn of 1464. They were visiting ruined temples and copying inscriptions 'here and there', playing music and drinking

wine as they went! Interestingly, Mantegna's huge classical paintings frequently incorporated stylish, gilded Roman capitals undoubtedly copied from such inscriptions.

Bartolomeo San Vito, also from Padua, revived and exploited the ancient capitals for his manuscripts, making a speciality of them. His Square capitals are elegant, expertly written and beautifully spaced. They follow the proportions of classical Roman inscriptions, yet are directly written with great freedom and confidence. The letters are alternately coloured and gilded in the manner typical of this scribe: line 1 (above) in red and gold; line 2, gold and green; line 3, purple and gold; line 4, gold and blue; and so on.

The pen angle is generally flattened, but there are many variations. A liberal use of pen manipulation (pen rotation and use of the pen corner) is needed in the formation of serifs, stem endings and flourishes. Like the classical inscriptions, words are randomly split at the end of lines. Occasionally, to achieve a 'fit', letters are written smaller (line 4, opposite) or compressed (line 11). Note the Greek form of **Y**; the tendency for **A,V** (and sometimes **M**) to have a backward lean; and San Vito's own very characteristic **R**.

S ISTE DISER

stodiat corpus regat. sensus erigat.
mores componat. actus probet. uo
ta et desideria mea perficiat. Cogi
tationes sanctas instituat. preteri
ta mala indulgeat. presentia emen
det. futura moderetur. Vitam ho
nestam et honorabilem mihi tribu
at. Et uictoriam contra omnes adu
sitates huius mundi. beatam pacē
spiritualem et corporalem mihi t
tribuat. Bonam spem caritatem t
fidem et castitatem humilitatem
et patientiam. Et quinq; sensus cō
poris mei regat et protegat. Septē
opera misericordię complere me
faciat. Duodecim articulos fidei.
Decem precepta legis firmiter cre
dere et tenere me faciat. Et a septē

The Hours of Eleonora. London, British Library, Yates Thompson Ms. 7 (a Book of Hours of the Virgin). Written by Matteo Contughi of Volterra, *c.*1480, probably in Urbino.

The page size is 8⅛" x 5½" (207 x 140 mm). The manuscript has 219 folios. The whole-page reproduction (actual size) and the enlargement (four times actual size) are both taken from folio 216v.

Early in the 15th century Humanist Scholars, having a strong aversion for the Gothic scripts of northern Europe, developed a 'new' script, the one that we now call Humanist minuscule. Its 'inventor', according to B L Ullman *(The Origin and Development of Humanistic Script),* was the scribe Poggio Bracciolini of Florence. The earliest known example is Poggio's manuscript of *De Verecundia* (Florence, Biblioteca Medicea-Laurenziana, Ms. Strozzi 96) which was written *c.*1402–1403. The text was corrected at the time by the author, Coluccio Salutati. Albinia de la Mare *(The Handwriting of the Italian Humanists)* suggests that Coluccio encouraged, and Niccolò Niccoli collaborated with Poggio. A manuscript begun by Poggio (Florence, Biblioteca Medicea-Laurenziana, Ms. Plut. 67. 15) contains pages of script attributed to Niccolò. For their inspiration these scholars studied the *litera antiqua,* Italian 12th-century Caroline minuscules (see *C9).* Niccolò actually owned at least one such 12th-century manuscript (see Introduction, *Fig. 6),* which is now in the collection of the British Library.

This Book of Hours was made for Eleonora Gonzaga,

who in 1509 became Duchess of Urbino. The scribe, Matteo Contughi, who signed the manuscript on folio 217R, probably completed the text *c.*1480. The illumination, however, was perhaps not completed until *c.*1520. It was mainly the work of Matteo da Milano, who, incidentally, also contributed to an Arrighi manuscript *(F5)* and probably also the Caraval Missal *(F1).*

The script is a delicate minuscule, very similar in character to many of the earlier Humanist minuscules written in Florence, such as those of Gherado del Ciriagio and Antonio Sinibaldi (see Alfred Fairbank, *A Book of Scripts,* plates 20 and 21). This lightweight 'Florentine' style is distinctively different from the more controlled minuscules of *F4* and *F5.* The arch shape of **m** and **n** is very curvy, and many letters are given long finishing strokes. There are, surprisingly, some instances of 'the biting of bows' (line 2, above) which is a *Gothic* trait (see *D3* notes).

The formation of **d, p, q** (and perhaps **b**), in which the bowls are made as almost complete o shapes, is a feature seen in some earlier scripts (see *C1,* and especially *C8).* Note that the **g** is of the Caroline minuscule type (compare the same letter in *F4* and *F5);* the **o** is nicely rounded; the foot serif on **r** is rather long; the use of short **s** is quite rare, even at the ends of words; and the waistline serifs are very heavy.

nris:& memorati testamenti
sui sancti Ius iurandu quod
iurauit ad abraham patre nrm:
daturum se nobis. Vt sine ti
more demanu inimico& nro&
liberati: seruiamus illi. In
sanctitate & iusticia coram ipo:
omnib'diebus nris. Et tu pu
er propha altissimi uocaberis:
preibis enim ante faciem dni
parare uias eius. Ad danda3
scientiam salutis plebi eius:in
remissionem peccatoru nro&
Per uiscera misericordie dei

omnes angeli euis: l

m omnes uirtutes e

date eum sol & luna

eum omnes stelle &

date eum celi celoru

London, British Library, Yates Thompson Ms. 6 (a Book of Hours of Roman Use). Written in Naples by Brother Alexander of Florence in 1477, for Joachinus Guasconus.

The page size is 5⅝" x 4" (142 x 103 mm). The manuscript has 192 folios. The whole-page reproduction (actual size) is taken from folio 172v, and the enlargement (five times actual size) from folio 31r.

Many of the earliest Humanist minuscules are ill-formed, and rather loosely written, so they lack coherence. Some of the later scripts, perhaps influenced by the uniformity of printed texts, suffer from being too precise. Their very consistency and precision, although extraordinary, actually detracts from that written quality which is vital in calligraphy. (See Stan Knight, *Varieties of Humanist Minuscule*.)

The scribe of this tiny manuscript, however, has written an extremely well-formed script, while maintaining a remarkable calligraphic rhythm and flow. The result is a minuscule which is attractive, clearly legible, and free from all mannerisms.

This Book of Hours was made for Joachinus Guasconus

of Florence – his name appears in three of the prayers, and his arms occur on folio 13r. The manuscript is signed and dated by the scribe, 'Bro. Alexander de florentia', who describes himself as 'a hermit of St Augustine'. There are two fully-illuminated pages, where even the text is gilded, and there are also many decorative initials throughout the manuscript.

The text on most pages is written in black and vermilion. The letters are rounded and broad, and the spacing is open (as required by the smallness of the script – larger scripts may be written closer), and very even. Note the 'beaked' serifs on the ascenders; the abrupt terminations at the base of **m** and **n**; the two forms of **q** and **s** – the short **s** being used only at word endings.

The large, coloured initials in the text are Square capitals; the 'filigree' line decorations are in a contrasting colour.

et propha altissimi uocaberis:

91

ros angeloᵣ̃ :et per omnes uirtutes cęlorum ̷ prĩ=
cipatus et poteſtates:thronos et dñationes:che=
rubin et ſeraphin deo patri obedientes:et ipſuᵣ̃
ſemper laudantes et glorificantes in ſęcula ſęcu=
lorum Amen. Alia coniuratio

Coniuro te diabole per oẽs ſc̃os ueteris
teſtamenti qui ſunt in paradiſo:et in
gloria dei patris õĩpotentis:et per glorioſam uir=
ginem mariam ̷ que ſuit uirgo ante partũ:ĩ par=
tu:atq̅ poſt partum:et concepit dñum noſtruᵣ̃
ieſum xp̄m ſaluatorem et redemptorem mũdi:
et per oẽs ſc̃os patriarchas et prophetas:apl̃os
euangeliſtas:martyres ̷ confeſſores ̷ doctores et
uirgines:et per omnes uirtutes dei ꞇe coniu=
ro ̷ ut non habeas poteſtatem ̷ neq̅ licentiã ſtan=
di in corpore famuli dei.N. quia deus fecit eum
ad ſimilitudinem ſuam:nec te lateat ſathana et
beelzebub ĩminere penas et tormenta quę uenĩ=
ent tibi in die iudicii ̷ et in diem ſempiternum:
quando deus uenturus eſt iudicare uiuos et mor=
tuos uelut clibanus ardens in terra:et uniuerſis
ſociis tuis et angelis malignis:in ſinum uadas:
et proinde intus dãnatus per infinita ſęcula ſę=
culorum . A   M   E   N

.

Sedente Leone.X.Pont.Maximo
Ludouicus Vicentinus Scribebat Romæ An.
Sal. M D X X .

us autem facerdos f

Quid adhuc defide

niam. Quid uobis u

nauerunt eum esse

n conspuere eum: et

The Medici Missal. Berlin, Staatsliche Museen zu Berlin, Kupferstichkabinett, Hs. 78. D. 17 (a Missal of Roman Use). Written in Rome in 1520 for Cardinal Guilio de' Medici (who later became Pope Clement VII) by Ludovicus Vincentinus, a scribe more familiarly known to us as Arrighi. The manuscript was illuminated, at least in part, by Matteo da Milano (see also *F1* and *F3).*

The page size is 15" x 10⅜" (380 x 263 mm). The manuscript has 408 folios. The whole-page reproduction is taken from folio 404v and the enlargement (three times actual size) from folio IIIR (part of Mark, chapter 14).

There are only two manuscripts surviving which are signed and dated by Arrighi, this one and one in Amsterdam (Universiteitsbibliotheek, Ms. II. A. 19). However, at least 15 manuscripts are attributed to him (see, Clough, 1988), including one in the British Library, Royal Ms. 12. C.viii *(F6)*, and a manuscript discovered by Vera Law in 1977, containing speeches of Giovanni Battista Gargha. The Gargha manuscript is the only other one of these to be written in Humanist minuscules. It was attributed to Arrighi by Vera Law after detailed comparison with this Berlin Missal.

The introduction of printing into Europe in the 15th century was to bring to an end the very long tradition of copying books by hand. Eventually, the scribe was to become obsolete. One positive aspect of this technological revolution,

however, was that the first printers were anxious to retain the appearance of the manuscript book and so scribes were employed in illuminating and rubricating the printed pages. Early printers derived both their page layouts and their typefaces from the work of contemporary scribes. In contrast to the 'blackletter' types used in Mainz, Venetian printers (like Nicolas Jenson and Aldus Manutius) based their type designs on Renaissance scripts. Modern Roman typefaces are the direct descendants of those Humanist letters.

From about 1523 Arrighi's main occupation in Rome was as a publisher. He had his own printing press, and he also designed at least three fine typefaces. Arrighi's script for the Missal perhaps betrays the influence of typography on the formation of his letters, especially his serifs. Those at the baseline and on the descenders are complex, requiring much use of pen manipulation and the pen corner (eg. see **i**, **m**, **n**, **s** and **x**).

Nevertheless, this is an expert script combining soundness of letter structure with good spacing. The **o** and related letters are round, and the arch shapes of **h**, **m**, **n**, and **u** are broad. The pen angle is generally very flat, except for making certain strokes in letters like **x** and capital **N**.

iefum xp̄m faluatorem et

hic (quod etiam ex eius scriptis, tãquã
ex animi sui imagine facile coniyci po=
test) nostræ tempestatis in rebus geren=
dis prudentissimus, omnibusqȝ discipli=
nis exornatus: Jn quem etiam illud om=
nium iudicio cadere uisum est, oratorȝ
omnium Jurisconsultissimum, Juriscon=
sultorum uero eloquentissimum extitis=
se. Qui, quantum fieri potuit, curaui
ut politissimis characteribus conscribe=
retur, Vt hoc ceu inuitamento quodã
addito ad legendum librum allicerere.
Ego uero fœlicissime mecum tunc actũ
putabo, si (quod spero) in legendo ope=
re, quod te delectet inueneris, auctorẽ
qȝ probaueris: Fieri nanqȝ istud non
posse putaui, sine animi erga te mei ƥ

o cadere uisum est, orat

risconsultißimum, Jurisc

ro eloquentißimum extu

antum fieri potuit, cura

is characteribus conscrib

London, British Library, Royal Ms. 12. C. viii (*Apologues* of Pandolfo Collenuccio). Written in Rome, probably before 1523, undoubtedly by Arrighi.

The page size is 8¼" x 5¼" (210 x 132 mm). The manuscript has 87 folios. The whole-page reproduction (actual size) and the enlargement (four times actual size) are both taken from folio 2v, part of the Address to King Henry VIII.

This manuscript is a luxury volume, specially commissioned from the scribe by Geoffrey Chamber as a gift for Henry VIII of England. It was illuminated by Attavante degli Attavanti of Florence. The title page is richly ornamented, displaying much use of matt and burnished gold. The margins, appropriately, are very generous.

The origins of Italic script can be seen in the rapid form of Humanist minuscules favoured by Niccolò Niccoli. Copies of classical texts made by this Renaissance scholar, *c.* 1420, are written in a script with cursive features – narrower letter forms, more forward slant and letters which join. This form of cursive Humanist script gained favour, and soon a more recognizable Italic style emerged, possibly first in the area surrounding Venice. By *c.* 1460 it had been adopted by the Papal Chancery for briefs and diplomatic correspondence

(hence 'Chancery Cursive' or *Cancellaresca Corsiva).*

The scribe, Ludovico degli Arrighi (surnamed Vincentino) neither signed nor dated this manuscript (unlike his Missal, *F5),* but there is little doubt about its attribution. Arrighi was a professional scribe, employed by the Papal Chancery from about 1519 to 1523, and a Writing Master. He was the first to publish an illustrated instruction book for writing the Chancery cursive style of Italic. *La Operina* is dated 1522 but it was probably not published until 1523 or 1524 (see Clough, 1988). It was reprinted in 1533. (Sigismondo Fanti's earlier Manual of 1514, contained only written guidance.)

The Corsiva script which Arrighi uses for this manuscript is extremely compressed, and its sharp, angular quality is emphasized by the rather steep pen angle and the strong forward slant. The **a** (and its related letters) and **o** are very pointed, as are the branches on **m**, **n**, and **u**. The ascenders and some descenders are long and hooked, but **p** and **q** have cross serifs. The short **s** occurs only at the end of words or in the **ss** ligature; **ct** and **st** are also ligatured. Note the typical, Humanist use of small, *upright* Square capitals as initials.

omnium Jurisconsultißimum, Juriscon=

95

Beatissima lei che morte ancise assai di qua dal natural confine Parranno

Allhor l'angeliche divise Et l'honeste parole, e i pensier casti Che nel cuor

Giovenil Natura mise Tanti volti che il tempo & morte han guasti Tornaranno

Allor più fiorito stato Vedrassi ove Amor tu mi legasti Tal ch'io à dito ne sarò

Mostrato Dirassi ecco colui che nel suo pianto Soura'l riso d'ogn'altro fu beato &

Amant^{mo} Beat^{mo} Car^{mo} Dign^{mo} Ecell^{mo} fra^{co} & Grat^{mo}

qgiadre · Donne in cui s'annida

nne seme tra noi d'alto ualore

nne che sete al secul nostro hor

s pregate deuote il uostro sole

Cambridge, Massachusetts, Houghton Library, Harvard University, Ms. Typ. 246 (a handwritten Specimen Book). Written in Siena in 1545, by Bernardino Cataneo.

The 'landscape' page size is 5¾" x 8¼" (145 x 210 mm). The manuscript has 20 folios. The whole-page reproduction is taken from folio 2v, and the enlargement (four times actual size) from folio 9R.

The reputation of the Writing Master Bernardino Cataneo rests on this single manuscript. No other example of his calligraphy has yet come to light. This outstanding exemplar of Renaissance scripts was written while Cataneo was teaching at the University of Siena. An ascription on folio 5R states, in Italian, that 'Bennardino (sic) Cataneo scrivea al Signor Odoardo Ralygh, Gentilhuomo Inglese'. An exact date, '4 February 1545' is given on folio 13R. The identity of the 'Edward Raleigh' for whom it was intended is uncertain, but there is evidence that a military observer of that name was in Milan in 1543.

This Specimen Book, in its original gold-tooled leather binding, contains 20 exemplars which are written only on the flesh side of each of the vellum leaves. The whole manuscript is reproduced as *An Italic Copybook,* and edited by Stephen Harvard. The texts were chosen to provide a different letter of the alphabet at the head of each page and these are arranged, more or less, in alphabetical sequence. Each of the initials like the **B** shown here, and those which begin

each line, are written in gold. At the foot of folios 2v, 3R, and 4v, a series of short words with elaborate Swash capitals are arranged in alphabetical order.

Cataneo provides, in his Copy Book, examples of two distinct forms of Humanist Italic script. On folios 12v, 17R, and 20v he demonstrates 'Formal Chancery' *(Cancellaresca Formata),* see also *F8* and *F9.* On all the other pages he shows the more ornate 'Chancery Cursive' *(Cancellaresca Corsiva).* Short colophons in the manuscript are written in a variety of hands – Gothic Rotunda, Square capitals or Humanist minuscules.

Cataneo's fine Corsiva, while just as compressed as Arrighi's *(F6),* is not quite so angular or pointed. Both are written with a strong forward slant, but Cataneo's hooked ascenders and descenders are perhaps longer. Arrighi's Corsiva, used for the text of an important book, is quite restrained. Cataneo, perhaps seeking to impress his student from England, indulges in a display of very ornate Swash capitals and exuberant flourishes. Nevertheless, his examples have been written slowly, with great care and precision. This is perhaps appropriate, for this Cataneo manuscript is the only one illustrated in *Historical Scripts* which was actually intended to be copied.

norte ancise assai di gua dal natural confine Parran

Se de le mie ricchezze care et tante
  Et si guardate; ond'io buon tempo uissi
  Di mia sorte contento, et meco dissi
  Nessun uiue di me piu lieto amante;
Io stesso mi disarmo: et queste piante
  A uezze a gir pur la; dou'io scoprissi
  Queglиocchi uaghi, et l'harmonia sentissi
  De le parole si soaui et sante;
Lungi da lei di mio uoler sen'uanno:
  Lasso chi mi dara Bernardo aita?
  O chi m'acquetera, quand'io m'affanno?
Morrommi: et tu dirai mia fine udita;
  Questi, per non ueder il suo gran danno,
  Lasciata la sua donna uscio di uita.

Signor, che parti et tempri gli elementi.
  E'l sole et l'altre stelle el mondo reggi.
  Et hor col freno tuo santo correggi
  Il lungo error de le mie uoglie ardenti;
Non lasciar la mia guardia, et non s'allenti
  La tua pieta; perch'io tolto a le leggi
  M'habbia d'amor, et disturbato i seggi,
  In ch'ei di me regnaua alti et lucenti.
Che come audace lupo suol de gli agni
  Stretti nel chiuso lor; cosi costui
  Ritenta far di me l'usata preda.
Accio pur dunque in danno i miei guadagni
  Non torni, e'l lume tuo spegner si creda;
  Confermo pie dipartimi da lui.

e audace lupo suol de gl

nel chiuso lor; cosi costu

ta far di me lusata preda

r dunque in danno i miei

London, Victoria & Albert Museum, Ms. L. 1347–1957 (Sonnets of Pietro Bembo in Italian). Written in Italy *c.* 1543 for Lisabetta Quirini, possibly on the instruction of the author, Cardinal Bembo.

The page size is 8½" x 5½" (215 x 140 mm). The manuscript has 79 folios, of which only the first 63 are written by the original scribe. The whole-page reproduction (actual size) and the enlargement (six times actual size) are both taken from folio 50v.

This style of Humanist Italic script is somewhat different from the Corsiva seen in *F6* and *F7*. In his *Libro nuovo d'imparare a scrivere* of 1540, Palatino describes it as *Cancellaresca Formata*. It is a much less dramatic hand than the Corsiva; it is more austere, more formal. The Formata script is written more slowly with a greater number of pen lifts. In appearance, it is not quite so compressed as the Corsiva, and its forms are more subtly rounded (especially in its arched shapes). Its ascenders and descenders are serifed and generally short. Ornamented Swash capitals, like those used with the Corsiva of Cataneo (see *F7*), are rather inappropriate for Formata Italic. This manuscript uses short, *upright* Square capitals, and they seem to be a better choice for its

more restrained script. These initial capitals are sensitively positioned in relation to the lines of text.

The Bembo manuscript, though small, is spaciously and most elegantly designed. Its margins are very wide, its interlinear space is generous, and its word spacing is close – all features which emphasize the lines of writing, and create an overriding sense of calm.

This incredibly small script retains its integrity even in enlargement. It is of very high quality and is free from excesses of any kind. On the one hand, it avoids the sharp angularity of many Corsiva scripts and, on the other, the mechanical rigidity of scripts which seek to imitate typographic precision. While it gives the impression of a smoothly flowing script, it has no joins, apart from the elegant ligatures (**sp** and **st**). Edward Johnston draws attention to the graceful tail on the letter **g**.

The letter spacing is open, as befits a tiny script (compare *F4* and *C5*). Larger versions of these letters could be written relatively closer together.

Il lungo error de le mie uoglie ardenti;

99

:. Bastarda grande llana :-

Obsecrote domina sancta

Maria mater Dei pietate

plenissima, summi regis fi-

lia, mater gloriosissima, m^a-

ter orphanorum, consola-

tio desolatorum, via erran-

tiuz

Fran^{co} Lucas lo escreuia en

Madrid año de M D LXX

Arte de Escrevir. London, Victoria & Albert Museum, 86. C. 107 (Wood-engraved Specimen Book by Francisco Lucas). The Lucas Manual was first published in Toledo in 1571 and the second, enlarged edition from which these illustrations are taken, was published in Madrid in 1577.

The page size is 7½" x 5½" (191 x 140 mm). The book has 96 folios. The whole-page reproduction (actual size) and the enlargement (one and three-quarters actual size) are both taken from folio 27R.

During the 16th century many wood-engraved writing manuals were produced. Despite the incredible skill of the engravers, the printed exemplars are inevitably removed from the feel of the original writing. Most of them compound the problem by cutting away the background of the block in order to simulate the appearance of black writing on white paper. Lucas minimizes the problem by making his letters large, and cutting the *letters* into the wood block.

Francisco Lucas is widely acknowledged as the finest of the Spanish Writing Masters. His *Arte de Escrevir* demonstrates that he is not only an excellent scribe, but also a consummate teacher. His written instructions are detailed and precise (he even gives certain measurements in pen-widths), and his wood-engraved exemplars are shown at three different sizes. The largest (shown here), most clearly reveals the construction of the letters; the smallest, gives the best sense of the flow of the writing.

In his Manual, Lucas provides exemplars for six writing styles – two forms of Chancery Italic, two types of minuscules, Gothic Rotunda and Square capitals. The major portion of the book is devoted to the 'Bastarda', which is the Spanish version of the Italian *Cancellaresca Formata* style (compare *F8*). They have the same elliptical, open letterforms. The only real difference is that Bastarda uses long, hooked ascenders. Lucas specifically recommends a wider body for the letters. Many Writing Masters advocating the Corsiva script, like Palatino in his 1540 Manual, suggested that the letters should be written just half as wide as their own height. This inevitably results in the more pointed letterforms characteristic of Corsiva (*F6*). In *Arte de Escrevir,* however, Lucas recommends that the letters should be written about two-thirds as wide as their own height. This extra width allows for a more open letterform, and encourages the gentle elliptical character of the Formata style.

The Bastarda script of Lucas is admirable for its clarity, its strength, and its lack of mannerisms. Alfred Fairbank considered it an excellent model for the development of a modern, formal Italic hand.

This script requires a steeper pen angle than that used in *F8*, especially for the fine branching strokes. Note the beautifully balanced lowercase **o**; the subtle arch forms of **m**, **n** and **u**; the pointed version of **v** (line 7); and the rare **z**.

...ug · Pius · cos · iīj · Trib · pot · ij · P. P. Aqueḋu·
ctum in nouis Athenis coeptum á Diuo hadri·
ano patre suo consummauit · dedicauitque ·

Apud Butrotum í Epyro Troia ·

C · Clodio Zosimo prī : & Iuliae Euterpe Matri · et · T ·
Pomponio Iuperco Suo Potine Monumentum
D · S · sibi et Suis fecit ·

Tragurie in Basilica virginis ex Muros ·

Imp · Caesar Diui · F · Aug · parens Coloniae
Murum · et Turris dedit ·

· Ibidem ·

T · Iulius optatus Turis vetustate consumptas
impensa sua restituit ·

Delphis in Templo Pythy Apollinis í pariete ·

ΘΕΟΙΣ ΕΠΙ ΑΡΙΣΤΑΓΟΡΑ ΑΡΧΩΝΤΟΣ
ΕΝ ΔΕΛΦΟΙΣ ΠΥΛΑΙΑΣ ΗΡΙΝΗΣ ΙΕ·
ΡΟΜΝΙΜΟΝΟΥΝΤΩΝ ΑΙΤΩΛΩΝ ΠΟ·
ΛΕΜΑΡΧΟΥ ΑΛΕΞΑΜΕΝΟΥ ΔΑΜΩΝΟΣ·

Ibidem ·

· ΠΥΘΙΝ ΜΑΝΤΙΣ ·

Ν ΑΥΘΕΣΩ ΑΥΚΟΕΡΓΕ ΕΜΟΝ ΠΟΤΙ ΠΙΟΝΑ·
ΝΗΟΝ ΣΗΝΙΦΙΛΟΣ ΚΑΙ ΠΑΣΙΝ ΟΛΥΜ.

De Notis Antiquis. London, Victoria & Albert Museum, Ms. L. 5161–1977 (Silloge of classical inscriptions by Publius Victor). Written in Italy *c.* 1500.

The page size is 11" x 8" (280 x 203 mm). The manuscript has 130 folios. The whole-page reproduction is taken from folio 81v (which includes two Greek inscriptions), and the enlargement (five times actual size) from folio 17v.

The Humanist scholars were primarily antiquarians. They were interested in ancient manuscripts and classical inscriptions, simply because they *were* ancient and classical. Such enthusiasm for antiquity led one group of scholars to study an old manuscript hand to create a 'new' one (see *F3* notes), and led another group to copy inscriptions 'here and there' (see *F2* notes). This book, recording ancient inscriptions from Rome, Italy and Greece, is an example of pure Humanism.

The manuscript, documenting Publius Victor's researches, is written in a superb Humanist cursive script by a relaxed, yet expert scribe. The generous margins and wide interlinear spaces, the assured layout of the page, and the beautifully written and spaced capitals suggest that he was trained in more formal calligraphy. James Wardrop found two other manuscripts written by this, as yet, unknown scribe. The first is in the Harvard University Library, Ms. Typ. 171. H (Hadrianus, *De Romanae Ecclesiae potestate*), written *c.* 1490; and the second in the Pierpont Morgan Library, Ms. 473 *(Liber censuum),* written *c.* 1510.

Edward Johnston, who once owned this manuscript, included reproductions of it in *Writing & Illuminating, & Lettering.* He suggested that it showed 'possibilities for an improvement in the ordinary present-day handwriting'. The manuscript eventually passed to James Wardrop who, heeding Johnston's words, actually modelled his own handwriting on this script.

The Silloge is written, very informally, with a rather blunt pen on good quality paper, using red and brown ink. It has a rhythmic consistency which stems from the excellent letter structure, the manual dexterity of the scribe, and the speed at which it was written. Note the nicely balanced initial capitals in the text and the natural letter joins. Many letters, such as **a** and **s**, have alternative forms.

Hystri tela manu iacientes sollicitabant.   Hinc Virgilius eun –
- dem locum de incluso Turno gratia elegantiore composuit.
Ergo nec clypeo iuuenis subsistere tantum
Nec dextra ualet: obiectis sic undique telis
O bruitur: strepit assiduo caua tempora circum
Tinnitu galea: & saxis solida aera fatiscunt.
Discussoq: uibre capiti: nec sufficit umbo
Ictibus: ingeminant hasti: & troes: & ipse
Fulmineus Menestheus: Tum toto corpore sudor
Liquitur: & piceum ⌐Nec respirare potestas⌐
Flumen agit: fessosquatit aeger anhelitus artus. Homerus ait.

FVRIVS IN QVARTO ANNALI.

ressatur pede pes: mucro mucrone: uiro uir. Hinc Virgilius ait:
Her& pede pes: densusq; uiro uir. Homeri est. Hunc secutus ho –
stius poeta in libro secundo belli hystrici ait. Non nisi mihi lin –
gue centum: atq; ora si etiam totidem uocesq; liquate. Hinc
Virgilius ait. Non mihi si lingue centum sint oraq; centum: Ho
merica descriptio est equi fugientis: in hęc uerba.

                                        Ennius hinc traxit.
Et cum sicut equus qui de presepibus actus
Vincla suis magnis animis abrupit: & inde

London, Victoria *&* Albert Museum, Ms. L. 1769 – 1952 (Macrobius, *Saturnalia).* Written in Rome and dated 14 August 1465.

The page size is 11¾" x 8" (299 x 203 mm). The manuscript has 150 folios. The whole-page reproduction is taken from folio 113R, and the enlargement (five times actual size) from folio 5R.

In addition to the high-grade, Humanist bookhands for copying classical or ecclesiastical texts, there were different cursive scripts available for legal or commercial purposes. Renaissance cursives evolved from earlier Gothic Chancery scripts, by adding Humanist features. They are rounded rather than pointed, and their well-spaced letters are written with many horizontal and diagonal joins. The form of **d** is upright, **g** has two complete bowls, and there is a strong preference for long **s**, even at word endings.

In a note on this Macrobius manuscript, James Wardrop considered it an example of 'the Humanistic cursive at its best, before it had become over-formalized'. He was never able to identify the scribe, but he did trace other manu-

scripts written by the same hand. These include two in the Vatican Library (Ms. Lat. 3232 and Ms. Lat. 3283) and one (which is probably another part of this V*&*A manuscript) in the Harvard University Library, Ms. Typ. 496 *(De Romanorum magistratibus* by Andrea Fiocchi).

This is a vigorous Humanist cursive, adapted for use as a book script by an accomplished scribe. What it lacks in overall consistency of letter formation and spacing, it makes up for in sheer liveliness and verve. Note the construction of the letter **d** (and sometimes, **p** and **q**), made like a complete letter o with the vertical stroke added (compare *C8* and *F3);* the short 'lead-in' stroke occasionally given to **a** and **q**; the flat top on **c**, especially when linked; the very distinctive, if rather 'loose' form of **g**; and the unusual serifs which are added to the ascenders. Ligatures are used to join **st** and **ct**, but many other more unusual combinations following long **s** can be seen – **se**, **si**, **sp**, **su** and even **ssi** and **sse**.

105

Glossary

Ascenders The strokes of certain letters which project above the line of writing, eg. b, f, h.

Benedicite Church canticle, commonly called, The Song of the Three Children. It begins, in Latin, *Benedicite omnia opera*, 'All ye works of the Lord, bless ye the Lord'.

Benedictional A book of liturgical Episcopal blessings.

Bi-folium Two folios, joined, making four pages.

Blackletter Typographic term for Gothic-style letterforms.

Branch, Branching Terms describing the thin, diagonal linking strokes of letters such as a, m, n, and u, especially in Humanist Italic scripts.

Canticle Ancient Church hymn, often using words from the Bible. Latin, *canticum*, 'song'.

Caroline, Carolingian Related historically or calligraphically to the period of Charlemagne and his successors.

Cartulary A collection of charters, most commonly grants of property rights or deed.

CLA Acronym for *Codices Latini Antiquiores*, a palaeographical survey by E A Lowe (see Bibliography).

Clubbed Strokes, usually ascenders, which are thickened.

Codex A manuscript in book form, made up of gathered quires, sewn together.

Colophon Tailpiece or summary at the end of a manuscript or one of its parts. Sometimes treated decoratively.

Compound Term describing letters built up with multiple strokes of the pen, eg. Versal capitals.

Compression, Lateral The narrowing of letterforms and spacing. Typical of certain scripts like Gothic and Italic.

Counterchange The reversal or interchange of colours, like that used when Versal capitals are decorated with filigree.

Cursive In calligraphy, an informal script written quickly, often with joins (eg. Chancery Cursive); everyday handwriting. Latin, *curso*, 'to run'.

Descenders The strokes of certain letters which fall below the writing line, eg. g, p, y.

Display Capitals A typographic term referring to the larger letters used for titles and headings; capitals similarly used in manuscripts.

Entasis An optical adjustment applied to a series of vertical lines. In architecture, the middle of columns swell outwards slightly. In lettering and calligraphy, the middle of letter strokes curve inwards a little.

Epigraphic Pertaining to inscriptional letters carved in stone, or engraved in metal. Greek, *epigraphē*, 'to write upon'.

Episcopal Pertaining to a Bishop of the Church. Greek, *episcopos*, 'an overseer'.

Exemplar A written or printed model for copying.

Explicit A written phrase in a manuscript denoting the end of a main section of text. Latin, *explicitus*, 'unrolled'. In the absence of page numbers, the explicits and incipits of a book are often used to identify a particular text.

Extant A manuscript or artefact known to exist. Latin, *extare*, 'to be visible'.

Flourish A decorative extension to a letterform.

Filigree Delicate tracery of fine lines.

Folio One leaf of a book. Two pages, one recto (right hand) and one verso (left hand).

Foundational Hand The basic script Edward Johnston developed from an English 10th-century manuscript, the Ramsey Psalter, which he considered to be 'an almost perfect model for a modern formal hand'.

Gloss A manuscript translation or comment, often written between the main lines of text.

Gilding The application of pure gold or silver, in powder or leaf form, to the manuscript page. The brightest manuscript gilding is the result of laying gold leaf onto a raised gesso (a plaster-based size), and burnishing.

Gospels The first four books of the New Testament, written by the Evangelists Matthew, Mark, Luke and John, recording the life of Christ. From the Anglo-Saxon, *godspell*, 'good news'.

Gothic Of the Goths. Originally coined in 16th-century Italy, as a term of derision for what was perceived as the 'barbaric' art of northern and western Europe. In calligraphy, refers to script styles commonly used during the late 12th to late 15th centuries.

Half-uncial Bookhand in common use during the 5th–8th centuries, with fully formed ascenders and descenders. Some of its letterforms are similar to those used in later minuscule scripts.

Hierarchy In medieval manuscripts, the arrangement of the various decorations or script styles in order of importance. For example, in many Carolingian manuscripts a section of text starts with a large decorative initial. This is followed by a few words in Roman capitals and then a section in Uncial script – which can be as little as one line or take up a whole page. The main body of the text is written in Carolingian minuscule and the explicits in Rustic capitals.

Historiated Term describing initial letters decorated with human figures, often recounting a story.

Hours, Book of Private prayer book for the daily use of the laity. Some were elaborately and expensively illuminated, according to the patron's position or wealth.

Humanist Of the Renaissance period. Term used especially of Italian scholars and scribes.

Illumination Originally, denoted the use of gold or silver to 'light up' the manuscript page. Now used in refererence to all kinds of manuscript decoration.

Incipit A written phrase in a manuscript, being the opening words of a main section of text. Latin, *incipere*, 'to begin'.

Initial The first letter of a word, sentence or paragraph, often distinguished by size, colour or decoration.

Insular Of the British Isles. Sometimes used if Anglo-Saxon or Irish origin is uncertain. Refers especially to such scripts of the 7th and 8th centuries.

Interlinear In calligraphy and typography, denotes the space between the lines of text.

Italic Indicating the scripts of Italian origin which are usually cursive and forward sloping.

Justification In typography, the spacing of words, and sometimes letters, to achieve text lines of equal length.

Ligature In calligraphy and typography, physically linked letterforms. Latin, *ligo*, 'to tie, to bind'.

Liturgical Pertaining to public worship, especially the form of words, or ceremonies, used in Church services. Greek, *leitourgia*, 'public service'.

Lombardic Term used by Edward Johnston and others to denote a heavy form of Gothic capital. Possible, if unlikely, connection with Lombardy in northern Italy.

Majuscules Formal letters of capital or uncial type.

Manipulation, Pen The act of rotating the angle, or changing the pressure of the pen while forming the letters.

Manuscript A book or other document written by hand. Latin, *manus*, 'hand'; *scribere*, 'to write'.

Medieval Related to the historical period from, roughly, the decline of the Roman Empire to the onset of the Renaissance. Latin, *medium aevum*, 'the middle age'.

Miniature Separate illustration painted in a manuscript. Now widely used to simply mean 'small painting'. Derives from Latin, *miniare*, 'to colour with red'.

Minuscules 'Small letters' as distinct from capitals, usually containing ascenders and descenders. In typography they are termed lowercase letters.

Monoline Term applied to letters where all the strokes are of the same thickness.

Offset In palaeography, the print of an ancient manuscript transferred, accidentally, onto another sheet.

Palaeography The study of ancient writing and manuscript book production for linguistic and historical research.

Palimpsest A manuscript sheet where the original text has been erased to allow a new one to be written over.

Papyrus A reed once common in Egypt. Hence, also, the writing material made from it. The first form of paper.

Parchment Animal skin prepared for writing. Now, often specifically relates to sheepskin.

Pen angle The position of the broad-edged pen in relation to the horizontal writing line. A 'natural' pen angle is where the thin stroke is at a generally consistent slope, for example 30° or 40°. A 'flattened' pen angle is where the thin stroke is generally parallel to the writing line. A 'floating' pen angle is where there are changes of angle within the script.

Pilcrow A decorative form of the Greek letter pi (Π), traditionally used in both manuscripts and printed books, to signify the beginning of paragraphs.

Pontifical A liturgical book containing services to be administered exclusively by the Pope or a Bishop.

Prescissus Term used of certain Gothic scripts which have flattened or 'dished' lower terminations. Latin, *praeseco*, 'cut off'.

Psalter A book containing just the Book of Psalms from the Old Testament of the Bible. Various Canticles are sometimes included.

Quadrata Term used of certain Gothic scripts with a square or angular aspect. Latin, *quadratus*, 'squared'.

Quill A pen made from the wing feather of a large bird such as a goose or, in more recent times, a turkey. Note Latin, *penna*, 'a feather'.

Quire A 'gathering' of bifolia to make up one section (or signature) of a codex book. Usually, 4 or 5 bifolia (16 or 20 pages) make up one quire.

Recto The top side of a folio or leaf. Any right-hand page.

Reed A riverside plant, similar in appearance to bamboo. Hence, also, the pen cut from a reed.

Renaissance The period of intellectual and artistic revival, spanning the late 14th to late 16th centuries, marked by a renewal of interest in ancient, classical culture. French, *renâitre*, 'to be born anew'.

Rite Ecclesiastical liturgy. Latin, *ritus*, 'a ceremony'.

Roll A document in scroll form. The Jewish Torah for liturgical use is still written in this form.

Rotunda Term used of certain Gothic scripts with a rounded aspect. Latin, *rotundus*, 'circular'.

Rustic Capital Term denoting the early majuscule book script and inscriptional letterform. The name possibly derives from its apparently unsophisticated appearance.

Sarum Roman name for the city of Salisbury in England.

Scribe A calligrapher. One who writes manuscripts. In medieval times, usually a monk or nun in a religious order. From the 11th century onwards, many secular or lay persons were also professional scribes.

Scriptorium A workplace of a scribe or group of scribes.

Shading A typographic term, referring to the change from thick to thin aspects of the curved strokes of letters.

Serif The tiny stroke used to terminate letter strokes.

Silloge A collection or catalogue.

Size In the decoration of manuscripts, the medium used for adhering gold leaf or powder to the page.

Square Capital The term used for the formal majuscule book script and inscriptional letter of the classical period.

Swash Capital Flourished form of capital, especially used with the Chancery cursive script. Because of their ornate character they are best used just as initials.

Textura Term used of certain Gothic scripts with strong angular aspect and tight lateral compression. Latin, *textilis*, 'woven'.

Uncial Majuscule bookhand in common use during the 4th to 8th centuries. E A Lowe used the terms 'Artificial' to denote elaborate uncials of the Roman style, and 'Capitular' to denote the less formal style used for chapter headings and colophons.

Vellum Animal skin prepared for writing. Now, often specifically relates to calfskin and, perhaps, goatskin.

Versal Term originally used of capital letters which signify the first letters of verses or paragraphs. Now, refers to manuscript capitals built-up with multiple strokes of the pen. Usually reserved for initials, headings or colophons.

Verso The under side of a folio or leaf of a document. Any left-hand page.

Vulgate The Latin version of the Bible revised by St Jerome, which was completed by AD 405. Latin, *vulgare*, 'to make public, popular'.

Weight In lettering, the relationship between the width of the stroke and the overall height of the letter.

Select Bibliography

Palaeography

Anderson, D M: *The Art of Written Forms*, Holt, Rinehart and Winston, New York, 1969

Aris, Rutherford: *Explicatio Formarum Litterarum*, The Calligraphy Connection, St Paul, 1990

Bischoff, Bernhard (trans. Dáibhí Ó Cróinín and David Ganz): *Latin Palaeography, Antiquity and the Middle Ages*, Cambridge University Press, Cambridge, 1990. Originally published Berlin, 1979 as *Paläographie des romischen Alterums und des abendländischen Mittelalters*

Bishop, T A M: *English Caroline Minuscule*, Oxford University Press, Oxford, 1971

Boyle, Leonard E: *Medieval Latin Palaeography*, University of Toronto Press, Toronto and London, 1984

Brown, Michelle: *A Guide to Western Historical Scripts from Antiquity to 1600*, British Library, London, 1990

Brown, Michelle: *Anglo-Saxon Manuscripts,* British Library, London, 1991

Brown, T Julian (ed. Janet Bately, Michelle Brown and Jane Roberts): *A Palaeographer's View: Selected Writings of Julian Brown*, Harvey Miller, London, 1993

Clough, Cecil H: 'A Manuscript of Paolo Giovio's "Historiae sui Temporis, Liber VII"; More light on the career of Ludovico degli Arrighi', an article in *Periodico della Società Storica Comense*, volume 53, Estratto, 1988–1989

Degering, H: *Lettering*, Pentalic, New York 1965 (originally published London, 1929)

de Hamel, Christopher: *Scribes and Illuminators*, British Museum Press, London and University of Toronto Press, Toronto, 1992

de la Mare, A C: *The Handwriting of Italian Humanists*, printed at the University Press, Oxford, for L'Association Internationale de Bibliophilie, Paris, 1973 (first of 2 volumes, the second in preparation)

Diringer, David: *The Alphabet*, 3rd edition, Hutchinson, London, 1968 (2 volumes: 1 text, 2 illustrations)

Fairbank, A and R W Hunt: *Humanistic Script of the 15th and 16th Centuries*, Bodleian Library, Oxford, 1960

Fairbank, A and B Wolpe: *Renaissance Handwriting*, Faber and Faber, London, 1960

Ganz, David: 'The Pre-conditions for Caroline Minuscule', article in *Viator*, volume 18, University of California Press, Berkeley, 1987

Ganz, David: 'The Carolingian Bibles from Tours', article in *The Early Medieval Bible*, Cambridge, 1994

Harvard, Stephen: *An Italic Copy Book: the Cataneo Manuscript*, Taplinger (for Harvard University and the Newberry Library), New York, 1981

Knight, Stan: 'Varieties of Humanist Minuscule', article in *The Scribe*, no. 33, London, 1985

Knight, Stan: 'Scripts of the Grandval Bible', 3-part article in the *The Scribe*, nos. 44, 45, 48, London, 1988, 1989, 1990

Knight, Stan: 'Versals Redefined', article in *Letter Arts Review,* volume 12, no. 1, Oklahoma, 1995

Knight, Stan: 'The Roman Alphabet', article in *The World's Writing Systems*, ed. Peter T Daniels and William Bright, Oxford University Press, New York, 1996

Lowe, E A: *Codices Latini Antiquiores*, Oxford University Press, 1934–1972
  1 The Vatican, 1934
  2 Great Britain, 1935 and 1972
  3 Italy, 1938
  4 Italy, 1947
  5 Paris, 1950
  6 France, 1953
  7 Switzerland, 1956
  8 Germany, 1959
  9 Germany, 1959
  10 Austria, Belgium, Czechoslovakia, Denmark, Egypt, Holland, 1963
  11 Hungary, Luxembourg, Poland, Russia, Spain, Sweden, USA, Yugoslavia, 1966
  12 Supplement, 1971

Lowe, E A: *English Uncial*, Oxford University Press, 1960

Lowe, E A (ed. Ludwig Bieler): *Palaeographical Papers, 1907–1965,* Oxford University Press, 1972 (2 volumes)

Milne, H J M and T C Skeat: *The Codex Sinaiticus and the Codex Alexandrinus*, British Museum, London, 1951

Morison, Stanley: 'Early Humanistic Script and the First Roman Type', article in *The Library*, fourth series, 24: 1–29, 1943

Morison, Stanley: *Politics and Script*, Oxford University Press, 1972

Ogg, Oscar: *Three Classics of Italian Calligraphy*, Dover Publications, New York, 1953

Osley, A S (ed.): *Calligraphy and Palaeography*, Faber and Faber, London, 1965

Osley, A S: *Mercator,* Faber and Faber, London, 1969

Osley, A S: *Luminario,* Milano Publishers, Nieuwkoop, The Netherlands, 1972

Osley, A S: *Scribes and Sources*, David Godine, Boston, 1980

Parsons, P J: 'Elegiacs by Gallus from Qaṣr Ibrîm', article in the *Journal of Roman Studies*, Volume 69, 1979

Rand, E K: *A Survey of the Manuscripts of Tours*, Medieval Academy of America, Cambridge, Massachusetts, 1929

Thompson, E M: *Handbook of Greek and Latin Palaeography*, Ares Publishers, Chicago, 1975 (originally published 1893)

Ullman, B L: *Ancient Writing and Its Influence*, MIT Press, Cambridge, Massachusetts, 1969 (originally published Longmans Green, New York, 1932)

Ullman, B L: *The Origin and Development of Humanistic Script,* Edizioni di Storia e Letteratura, Rome, 1960 and 1974

Wardrop, James: *The Script of Humanism,* Oxford University Press, 1963

Wardrop, James: 'Civis Romanus Sum: G B Palatino and his circle', article in *Signature*, New Series 14, 1952

Watson, Andrew G: *Catalogue of Dated and Dateable Manuscripts c. 700–1600 in the Department of Manuscripts in the British Library*, British Library, London, 1979 (2 volumes: 1 text, 2 plates)

Watson, Andrew G: *Catalogue of Dated and Dateable Manuscripts c. 435–1600 in Oxford Libraries*, Oxford University Press, 1984 (2 volumes: 1 text, 2 plates)

Webber, Teresa: 'The Script of the Eadwine Psalter', article in *The Eadwine Psalter: Text, Image and Monastic Culture in Twelfth-Century Canterbury*, ed. by Margaret Gibson, T A Heslop and Richard W Pfaff, The Medieval Humanities Research Association, volume 14, London, 1995

Inscriptions

Catich, E M: *The Trajan Inscription in Rome*, Catfish Press, Davenport, 1961

Cook, Brian: *Greek Inscriptions*, British Museum Publications, London, 1977

Evetts, L C: *Roman Lettering*, Pitman, London, 1938 and 1955 (now published by A & C Black)

Gordon, Arthur E: *Latin Epigraphy*, University of California Press, Berkeley, Los Angeles and London, 1983

Grasby, Richard: 'The Making of Two Roman Inscriptions', 2-part article in *The Scribe*, nos. 56, 57, London, 1992, 1993

Hayes, James: *The Roman Letter*, Lakeside Press, R R Donnelley, Chicago, c. 1968

Perkins, Tom: 'The Trajan Secrets', article in *The Edge*, volume 2, issue 5, London, 1997

Victoria & Albert Museum: *Roman Lettering*, HMSO, London, 1958

Calligraphy

Child, Heather (ed.): *The Calligrapher's Handbook*, A & C Black, London and Taplinger, New York, 1985

Fairbank, A: *A Book of Scripts*, Faber and Faber, London, 1977 (first published as a King Penguin, London, 1949)

Fairbank, A: *A Handwriting Manual*, Faber and Faber, London, 1932 and 1978

Gray, Nicolete: *Lettering as Drawing*, Oxford University Press, 1970 (2 volumes: 1 The Moving Line, 2 Contour and Silhouette)

Gray, Nicolete: *A History of Lettering*, Phaidon, London and David Godine, Boston, 1986

Gullick, Michael: *Calligraphy*, Studio Editions, London, 1990

Hewitt, Graily: *Lettering*, Seeley, Service, London 1954

Jackson, Donald: *The Story of Writing*, Studio Vista, London 1981; now from the Calligraphy Centre, Monmouth

Johnston, Edward: *Writing & Illuminating, & Lettering*, Hogg, London, 1906; then Pitman, London; now published by A & C Black, London

Johnston, Edward (ed. Heather Child): *Formal Penmanship*, Lund Humphries, London, 1971

Johnston, Edward (ed. Heather Child and J Howes): *Lessons in Formal Writing*, Lund Humphries, London, 1986

Woodcock, John (with historical notes by Stan Knight): *A Book of Formal Scripts*, A & C Black, London and David Godine, Boston, 1992

Illumination

Alexander, J J G: *The Decorated Letter*, Thames and Hudson, London, 1978

Alexander, J J G: *Insular Manuscripts, 6th to the 9th Century*, (A Survey of Manuscripts Illuminated in the British Isles, volume 1), Harvey Miller, London, 1978

Alexander, J J G: *Medieval Illuminators and their Methods of Work*, Yale University Press, New Haven, 1992

Backhouse, Janet: *The Illuminated Manuscript*, Phaidon, Oxford, 1979

Backhouse, Janet: *The Lindisfarne Gospels*, Phaidon, Oxford, 1981

Brown, Michelle: *Understanding Illuminated Manuscripts, a Guide to Technical Terms*, British Library, London and Malibu, 1994

d'Ancona, P and E Aeschlimann: *The Art of Illumination*, Phaidon, Oxford, 1969

de Hamel, Christopher: *A History of Illuminated Manuscripts*, Phaidon, London, 1986 and 1994

Donovan, Claire: *The Winchester Bible*, British Library, London and Winchester Cathedral, 1993

Henry, Françoise: *The Book of Kells*, Thames and Hudson, London, 1974 and 1976

Kauffmann, C M: *Romanesque Manuscripts, 1066–1190*, (A Survey of Manuscripts Illuminated in the British Isles, volume 3), Harvey Miller, London, 1975

Marks, Richard and Nigel Morgan: *The Golden Age of English Manuscript Painting*, Chatto and Windus, London, 1981

Morgan, Nigel: *Early Gothic Manuscripts, 1190–1285*, (A Survey of Manuscripts Illuminated in the British Isles, volume 4), Harvey Miller, London, 1982 and 1985

Mütherich, Florentine and Joachim Gaedhe: *Carolingian Painting*, Chatto and Windus, London, 1977

Nordenfalk, Carl: *Celtic and Anglo-Saxon Painting*, Chatto and Windus, London, 1977

Oakeshott, Walter: *The Two Winchester Bibles*, Oxford University Press, 1981

Sandler, Lucy F: *Gothic Manuscripts, 1285–1385*, (A Survey of Manuscripts Illuminated in the British Isles, volume 5), Harvey Miller, London, 1987

Temple, Elżbieta: *Anglo-Saxon Manuscripts, 900–1066*, (A Survey of Manuscripts Illuminated in the British Isles, volume 2), Harvey Miller, London, 1976

Weitzmann, Kurt: *Late Antique and Early Christian Book Illumination*, Chatto and Windus, London, 1977

Wright, David H: *The Vatican Vergil, a masterpiece of Late Antique art*, University of California Press, Berkeley, 1993

Exhibition catalogues

Bodleian Library: *Manuscripts at Oxford, an exhibition in memory of Richard William Hunt*, ed. A C de la Mare and B C Barker-Benfield, Bodleian Library, Oxford, 1980

British Museum: *The Golden Age of Anglo-Saxon Art, 966–1066*, ed. Janet Backhouse and D H Turner, London, 1984

Central School of Art and Design: *The Art of Lettering and the March of History*, ed. Nicholas Biddulph and Nicolete Gray, London, 1982

Victoria & Albert Museum, London: *The Universal Penman*, ed. J I Whalley and V Kaden, HMSO, London, 1980

Walters Art Gallery: *Two Thousand Years of Calligraphy*, ed. D E Miner, V I Carlson and P W Filby, Baltimore, 1965

Indices

110

COLOPHON

Book design by Stan Knight
Typography by Marcia Friedman

The text face is 10½ on 12 point Adobe Garamond
with Adobe Garamond Expert Set & Minion Greek
all designed by Robert Slimbach

Special Greek sort created by LL